CHARLI PERSIP
HOW NOT TO PLAY DRUMS

Not for drummers only

Newly revised and expanded to include "The Warm Up Exercise"

Second Floor Music

Book design: **Maureen Sickler**
Cover design: **John Bishop, OriginArts**
Cover photo: **Todd Bishop**
Charli Persip biography: **Tom Nuccio**
Photos of Mr. Persip: **Shawn Walker, PhotoArts Studio**
Music Engraving: **Osho Endo**
A DON SICKLER PRODUCTION
Copyright © 1987, 2003 Second Floor Music
130 West 28th Street, NY, NY 10001 USA

CHARLI PERSIP
HOW NOT TO PLAY DRUMS
Not for drummers only

Newly revised and expanded

About Charli Persip *4*

Introduction *6*

1. **Some Little-Known Facts About The Traps** *9*
2. **Give Your Drummer A Break** *12*
3. **Productive Practicing Procedures** *14*
4. **Exploring The Validity Of Rudimental Training And Practice** *16*
5. **Reading Music** *20*
6. **The Importance Of Good Health Habits, Mental And Physical** *24*
7. **Hints On Tuning, Maintenance And Equipment** *26*
8. **Keeping Time** *30*
9. **The Art Of Listening** *33*
10. **The Art Of Accompaniment** *34*
11. **Discussing Ensemble Accompaniment** *36*
12. **The Warm Up Exercise** *40*
    Bass Drum And Hi-Hat Patterns *51*
    Introducing The Flam *52*
    Study In Flam Continuity *53*
    Suggested Flam Sticking *54*

SECOND FLOOR MUSIC 130 West 28th Street, NY, NY 10001 USA   www.secondfloormusic.com

Charli Persip

During a 50 year career that's still going strong, Charli Persip has served as a textbook example of how to play the drums. He has proven his worth in a variety of jazz ensembles and handled the transitions from one group to the next without ever missing a beat.

Born in Morristown, New Jersey, Persip gained initial playing experience in Newark with tenorman Joe Holiday and an R & B combo fronted by Billy Ford. In 1953, he worked with Tadd Dameron before joining Dizzy Gillespie's big band later that year. Through a five year association with Gillespie (which ended when the group disbanded in 1958), Persip derived his first taste of public recognition and began to establish a solid reputation. His credentials expanded in the following year via freelance work with Johnny Richards, Phil Woods, Harry Edison, and Harry James.

Around 1959, Persip organized a powerhouse hard bop unit which featured some of today's jazz greats at early stages of their careers. Flaunting the youthful talents of Freddie Hubbard, Ron Carter, Ronnie Mathews and Roland Alexander, the drummer unveiled his band at Birdland and proceeded to document its music on an album for Bethlehem Records entitled *The Jazz Statesmen*.

The sixties brought on an assortment of projects which set his career into perpetual motion. In 1962, Persip accompanied French stage and screen star Yves Montand for two limited Broadway engagements and a West Coast tour. He spent the following three years as house drummer in the Apollo Theatre show band led by Reuben Phillips. Through this association, Persip gained a deeper insight into rock and roll playing by backing many well-known acts of the time, including the popular Motown performers. After a tour of Japan with fellow drummers Buddy Rich, Louis Bellson and Philly Joe Jones, Persip began a seven year stint in 1966 as drummer and assistant musical director for Billy Eckstine. During his tenure with Eckstine, he also presented drum clinics, lectures and seminars in such widespread locations as Houston, Boston and Sydney, Australia. In addition, he appeared as a sideman on numerous recordings led by everyone from Quincy Jones and Benny Golson to Nancy

Wilson and Cannonball Adderley.

After leaving Eckstine in 1973, Persip upheld a regular itinerary of educational activities including a strong involvement as drum instructor for New York's Jazzmobile program. He freelanced his way through the ensuing years with the likes of Archie Shepp, Frank Foster and the Collective Black Artists ensemble.

In 1980, the drummer teamed with trumpeter Gerry LaFurn to form a 17 piece orchestra that Persip named Superband. The band compiled a sparkling book of newly arranged standards and original compositions and made its recording debut on Stash Records. With the departure of LaFurn in 1983, Persip took over sole leadership of the band and recorded a second album entitled *In Case You Missed It* on the Soul Note label. Throughout the album, Persip demonstrates his unique and superior techniques for accompanying big bands and large ensembles. The most recent big band recording under Persip's leadership is *No Dummies Allowed*, recorded by Charli Persip and Supersound (also on Soul Note).

Along with Supersound, Persip keeps busy on the New York scene with a heavy agenda of freelance gigs, private teaching and clinic appearances. His current teaching engagements include the Mannes/New School Jazz Program and Queensborough Community College (C.U.N.Y.). As a clinician, Persip endorses Avedis Zildjian cymbals. A rare combination of tradition and innovation, Charli Persip remains an enduring force whose playing will always be in great demand.

Tom Nuccio

Mr. Persip's web site is www.charlipersip.com

Introduction

When I joined the Dizzy Gillespie Orchestra in 1955, I was young and very excited about joining that particular orchestra. It was my favorite large ensemble. Also, in my opinion, the Gillespie orchestra of the mid-40s into the 50s was the freshest and the greatest big band of the age. Of course, playing with Dizzy greatly spoiled me and I haven't changed a bit. Whenever one is caressed, one tends to be spoiled, and Mr. Gillespie's music had caressed me. Now, to be caressed by the greatest is a special way of being spoiled as it tends to make the spoilee aspire to the same great heights and achievements as the spoiler.

Because this was my favorite band, I had listened to it whenever possible, both on records and at live performances. Consequently, I knew all the arrangements by heart, so I was ready. Boy, was I ready . . . I thought. After the first show on the opening night, when we came off stage, Mr. Gillespie said to me, "It's really good. You're really getting it together." He continued, "You know what, now that you know what to play, you've got to learn what **not** to play."

learn what not to play

Dizzy's words made quite an impression on me. That incident, and many more like it, pointing up the validity of how not to do a thing as opposed to how to do a thing, stimulated the title and the basic subject matter of this book: **How Not To Play Drums.**

This is not a method book per se. There are many drum method books on the market nowadays that discuss how to play the instrument correctly, but from my own experience and observations, many problems drummers have can be helped by exploring how **not** to do a thing, as well as how to do it.

communication between musicians is vital

This book is meant to point up one of the most valuable learning experiences: communicating with experienced musicians. Those words of Dizzy's, along with conversations over the years with other musicians like Art Blakey, Kenny Clarke and Elvin Jones, did a great deal to shape the quality and consistency of my musicianship. So you could consider **How Not To Play Drums** as a rap session between Charli Persip and yourself—if you love the instrument enough to want to improve the way you listen to, perform with, and in the case of the aspiring drummer, play the instrument.

drummers are accompanists

this book is not for drummers only

As an instructor I lean heavily on teaching the aspiring drummer to be an accompanist. No matter how fast or technically adept a drummer is, if one is to play successfully with other musicians it is necessary to master the art of accompaniment, i.e., the ability to play compatibly with other musicians in various ensemble situations. In order to achieve this one must have a complete understanding of the function of this instrument. This book is designed to give the reader just that, a complete understanding of the traps or the set of drums. Because this complete understanding of the drum set is very helpful in enjoying, communicating and playing with drummers, I recommend this book for all musicians and lovers of the drum set.

Charli Persip

1

SOME LITTLE-KNOWN FACTS ABOUT THE TRAPS

(traps being a set of drums; or, as designated by Max Roach, the multiple percussion instrument)

drum set was developed for jazz

In order to master the drums, one should know the history of the drums. Fortunately, the history of the traps is synonymous with the history of jazz. When I realized that the traps were developed to play jazz and that it is the *only* instrument that was developed to play jazz, it filled me with a greater sense of pride to be involved with the instrument.

Jazz, in my conception, is music with a ritualistic rhythmic pulse or beat. In jazz music there is room for improvisation, but most importantly, jazz is music that was born out of the black or African-American experience in this country. Therefore, blues, gospel, rock, and other forms of rhythmic music are forms of jazz. Unfortunately today's connotation of jazz does not do justice to the true vastness of the music. In my opinion jazz should be called "rhythm and blues." The music is certainly rhythmic, and blues phrasing and the feeling of the blues is consistent throughout any jazz offering.

jazz is a spiritual inspiration

The blues is both happy and sad, highly indicative of black peoples' struggles and accomplishments in this society. Laughing to keep from crying is the basic message of the blues. Although jazz and the blues were developed by African-Americans, the feeling of the music is spiritually inspirational to *all* human beings. Therefore we can safely say that the music called jazz is a very beautiful and valuable cultural contribution to the world for all time.

The evolution of jazz parallels the development and evolution of the traps. We know from history that jazz came out of the street bands in and around the New Orleans area. When the enterprising entrepreneurs or producers of that time started putting the bands inside in more or less cabaret settings, where the bands played for shows as well as their own music, the traps were developed. Because to my knowledge there is no exact data or extensive documentation on when this development occurred, I think that reasons of economy brought it about.

Throughout the history of jazz economizing by minimizing the number of musicians in ensembles has been, and still is, practiced. Minimizing the number of musicians in ensembles is not always for financial economy. Sometimes it is for economy of space, because there are all sizes of rooms and areas (stages, etc.) where the music is produced. The street bands had at least three people playing instruments belonging to the drum family: one person playing bass drum, one playing snare, and one playing cymbals. It is my opinion that for the aforementioned reasons of economy the situation developed in which one drummer did what three had previously done, thus the emergence of the traps. A new instrument was born, an instrument invented to play jazz. An instrument where the player uses his entire body, all four limbs simultaneously, to make music. An instrument that is totally American, but belonging to a family of instruments deeply rooted in African culture.

the traps allowed one drummer to sound like three

A unique element of playing this instrument is the continuous use of the legs and feet, the drums being the only acoustic instrument that uses the entire body this way. This situation makes the seat, or drum throne, as it is commonly known, the most important piece of equipment in the drum set. In most performing situations you will be sitting from one to two hours without a break, with hands and feet in constant motion. This puts an exceptional strain on the back and pelvic area. Therefore, it is imperative to use a relatively soft but firm and very stable seat to prevent physical problems in later years.

the drum throne

One of the world's greatest existing misconceptions among drum lovers is which piece of drum equipment is the most important musically. I've already mentioned the importance of the drum seat physically. But whenever I ask aspiring drummers their opinion on which piece of equipment is the most important musically, I get votes for the snare drum, the ride cymbal, and the hi-hat. Very few, if any, choose the bass drum. In any African percussion ensemble there is a master drummer that plays a bass-type drum. In all marching bands the bass drum is the foundation of the beat.

bass drum is the foundation

Bass means bottom or foundation. We are all aware that without solid foundations, buildings would collapse. The same holds true in music. The bass notes are the foundation of any composition, any chord or chord progression. The bass drum has the same function in an ensemble where the traps are used. The

bass drum supports bass violin

bass drum rhythms should accompany or match what the bass violin plays. If the bass violin is playing a 4/4 rhythm, commonly known as straight ahead, the bass drum should play the same thing with a compatible volume. Many drummers, when playing the conception of jazz that utilizes 4/4 or straight-ahead rhythm from the bebop evolution, use the bass drum only for kicks or accents but keep no time with it. This is undesirable as it gives the bass violin no support. It is very difficult to make bass drum kicks and accents yet still keep a 4/4 beat that is light enough in sound so as not to overpower the bass violin, but this technique must be developed in mastering this instrument. All of the great masters, past and present, have this ability. In my opinion, the function of the bass drum in pop/rock music graphically points up the importance of the bass drum by the way the rhythms match so beautifully those of the electric bass.

hands off!

I had the privilege of doing a lecture/demo with the great Dizzy Gillespie some time ago, and he made a statement that demonstrated his feelings about the bass drum. I would like to interject at this point that Mr. Gillespie was a great exponent of the drums. He had a natural feel and love for the instrument and throughout his career he imparted many tips and suggestions that improved the playing of many of the legendary drummers of this era. Mr. Gillespie said that if he were teaching the drums, he would not allow his students to touch any hand drums for about two years, meaning that he would have his students work with the bass drum and accompanying hi-hat only for that long. Now I know that this sounds a bit extreme, and Mr. Gillespie does have a flair for the comedic and the bizarre, but all this not withstanding, his point for the importance of the bass drum is most certainly well made.

2
GIVE YOUR DRUMMER A BREAK
(or, don't dis your drummer)

Too many times we have bandleaders, composers, conductors, other tonal instrumentalists and vocalists trying to tell the drummer how to play. While there is nothing wrong in making suggestions to the drummer about how one may want a piece of music played or what rhythm may be desired, to try to tell drummers how to play their instrument is a no-no. Of course, in the case of an inexperienced student drummer any honest critique or suggestion on how to correct certain weaknesses may be in order.

give your drummer a chance

Have faith and confidence in your drummer. Allow your drummer to express his or her ideas and imagination as long as it is not a destructive force. In too many cases when the bandleader has a favorite drummer, they want their drummer to sound like that favorite drummer. If your favorite drummer is not available and you have to use the services of another accomplished drummer, give this drummer a chance to express his or her conception of the music before you come down on them. Keep in mind that harsh, tasteless and disrespectful critiques bring about tension that makes it impossible for the drummer to relax, and relaxation is the key to successfully playing this music.

In many cases your drummer, in playing something other than what you may want or that you hadn't thought of, may take the music to another level and **you** may learn something. For example, Miles Davis had one of the greatest groups in the history of jazz, featuring the drumming of the legendary Philly Joe Jones, who at that time was Miles' favorite drummer. However, when Tony Williams joined the group later, Miles did not expect Tony to play like Philly Joe: he allowed Tony freedom of imagination and let him develop his own conception of what Miles was playing. Consequently, a whole new rhythmic concept arose, and the rest is musical history.

keeping time is everyone's responsibility

Do not expect your drummer to keep time for you. If you need someone to keep time for you that's your weakness. The drummer's rhythmic conception and coloring of the time feeling should be enjoyable and inspirational to the ensemble. In making suggestions to your drummers, help them to learn, in a respectful manner, "how not to play" instead of how to play.

PRODUCTIVE PRACTICING PROCEDURES 3

practice

First, let me say that practicing is a completely necessary part of learning the instrument. **You must practice**, there's no question about it. Now there are some drummers who practice eight hours a day; there are other drummers who practice two hours a day; some practice one hour a day. The length of the practice session is not the most important factor. What is important is to have a daily, consistent practice program with maximum concentration.

be honest with yourself

As for the amount of time spent, practice only as long as you feel like working. That way your practice hours will be productive and rewarding.

be committed

Also, don't put time limits on your achievement goals. What counts is commitment. Many aspiring drummers have asked me if, with practice, they would achieve a certain goal in six months or one year or some other specific time limit. It is much better to say, "I am going to achieve my goal no matter how long it takes."

practice what you can't play

Don't spend the majority of your practice time playing what you already know or can play. It is all right to spend some time doing this as it is fun and helps stimulate and maintain confidence and that is important. But beware. Too much of this procedure will put you in danger of "ego tripping," which is a dangerous psychological situation for educational purposes. You will benefit far more by devoting the best of your practice time to improving and perfecting difficult situations and *things you cannot do*. The concentration and self discipline necessary to do this are vital steps to improvement.

use your body

. . . and your mind

There are two basic areas of practice: the **physical** includes rudiments and exercises to improve technique and flexibility. The second, and possibly more important, aspect of practice is the **development of your musical senses**. That includes reading, of course, and learning as much about music as possible. I will discuss exercises in both these areas in the next chapters.

Within the physical area of practicing, always maintain a feeling of rhythm. It's not a good practice for drummers to get

always keep time

so involved in the execution of exercises that they forget the importance of keeping time. I can't stress this too much—always think both musically and rhythmically when practicing. Of course, repetition is necessary when practicing exercises for flexibility and endurance, but don't allow the repetition and the quest for speed to dull your mind to the musical aspects of practice.

learn music theory, practice reading

After spending a productive amount of time in physical development, get involved with music theory and reading. I suggest that prospective drummers should have or should acquire some knowledge of the piano. It's been said by many musicians that every musician should have some knowledge of the piano, but it is particularly important for drummers. It could also be beneficial for drummers to be familiar with additional melodic instruments. There are many drummers who are multi-instrumentalists, but a lot of drummers are so dedicated to the drums that they find it difficult, if not impossible, to take the time to learn another instrument. They want to use all their practice time in trying to get the drums together. This was my problem, but I finally took the time to acquire a fundamental knowledge of keyboard and other melodic percussion instruments.

Keep in mind that the drum is not a melodic instrument per se. it can and should be played melodically utilizing the different tonal colors available from each drum, but it is basically a rhythm instrument.

don't always practice alone

Because the basic function of the drummer is to accompany other musicians in ensemble situations, practicing with a metronome, click track (if available), and recorded material is advisable. If possible, try to get together with other musicians in playing situations. This will bring about improvement in the most important area of development—listening. I know in a lot of communities it's hard for the young musicians to get together, but it can be done. It's all a matter of how much you want to do it. I hear a lot of musicians say, "I really wish there was a place where I could go and play." Instead of wishing, there are practical ways of getting rehearsal space: for very small fees in most towns you can rent studios. If three or four musicians contribute, reasonably-priced studio space is available. It's also of great value to play with experienced professional musicians whenever possible, although I don't recommend this for beginners.

you can find rehearsal space

EXPLORING THE VALIDITY OF RUDIMENTAL TRAINING AND PRACTICE

The teaching of rudiments has become a controversial subject with many teachers and aspiring drummers. Years ago every teacher taught the 26 rudiments religiously and it is still an effective way to develop technique. Over the years some teachers have begun to to eliminate extensive rudimental study because of the tendency of students to get too rudimental in their thinking. Also, the music of the rudiments was also the music of the military—marches, etc.

practicing rudiments is physical training

I agree that one can become too rudimental, at the expense of musical creativity, but that can be overcome by proper thought and concentration while studying rudiments. **The most important thing is to think and play musically**. Rudiments are just exercises, but they are good exercises. With a thorough knowledge of rudiments, you'll know just about every way to strike the drums effectively. Rudiments cover practically every combination of double and single sticking, as well as some triple sticking. Consequently, a good knowledge of rudiments will provide the physical ability to play just about anything that comes into your mind.

using rudiments is mental training

invert the rudiments

Some drummers get so involved with rudimental practice that when performing, they play rudiments instead of creative rhythmic and melodic statements. Like "I'll play a paradiddle here or a roll here," instead of trying to play a rhythmic or melodic line that uses the roll or the paradiddle as a musical element. To avoid "fixation" on rudiments, try this: once you've learned a rudiment in its basic form, turn it around and experiment with what might be called inversions, or different ways of playing it. With the paradiddle, for instance, first learn to play it in its "pure" form, with no accents. Then try accenting the first beat. Next, try accenting the second beat, then the third and then the fourth. While you're doing this, try to listen to the sound of the shifting accents combined with the steady rhythm of the paradiddle. This will help you to maintain a musical feeling.

Another interesting and very musically enlightening way of

play rudiments with 2 different pitches — practicing rudiments is to use two drums of different pitches, one for each hand. You will hear every tone when you produce the pitches correctly. This technique will give you practice in hearing intervals, since you can change the pitches of the two drums. In addition, it will lay the groundwork for developing the ability to compose rhythmic and melodic phrases based on the tones of the various drums in the kit—a musical approach to accompaniment that is quite different from the common practice of moving around the set in a physical manner and accepting what comes out.

practice rudiments in time — Right from the beginning, practice rudiments in time. Start at a very slow tempo, of course, so the muscles can memorize the necessary coordination. Gradually go to faster tempos only after previous tempos have been perfected. By perfecting tempos I mean being completely relaxed while achieving an even sound. Inspiring the time feeling within the ensemble is a major function of the drummer, and perfecting the rudiments **in time** gives the drummer practice in that function. Even when playing free jazz today one must be aware of time, be able to play in time and have good time.

play along with recordings — One way to make practicing rudiments and rhythms fun is to play along with recordings, either one of your favorite records that has a good tempo or a click track or drum machine. Practice the various rudiments along with the record, while trying to keep a good musical feeling. This helps make rudimental practice interesting and creative. Keep in mind that rudiments are exercises to strengthen muscles and increase skill and technique, not ends in themselves.

use hands + feet
practice rudiments with hands + feet — Rudiments should be used in developing hand **and** foot technique. Just as you practice with the sticks—right, left, right, left, left right, right right, left left, and so on—practice the same rudiments with your feet—right foot, left foot, etc. Then use both hands and feet together—(foot) right right, (stick) right right, (foot) left left, (stick) left left—first in simple combinations, then increasing in complexity—(foot) right, (foot) left, (stick) right (stick) left, and so on. Practice the same rhythms, but spread them over the entire instrument. This practice technique should increase coordination and keep you creative and challenged at the same time.

Remember, it is very important to **play in time**, and the more you practice in time, the more likely you'll play in time.

So many of us are in a hurry today—hurry to get through

learn speed slowly

practice, hurry to be a professional—that we don't like to play slowly. The discipline of practicing slowly is an essential part of getting yourself and your instrument together. Take your time. Don't be afraid to start slow—it's easier to play an exercise slowly. You have a chance to be more relaxed at a slow tempo, and being relaxed is very important. Learn to discipline yourself to be relaxed when you practice and when you play—take your time, listen to what you're doing, listen to what the other musicians are doing. Speed will come naturally as your muscles and brain become familiar with the patterns you're playing.

There is a tendency among some drummers to equate speed with technique, and those drummers like to show how fast they can play, often without regard to musicality. But speed is only a tool to be used when appropriate. You have to have it, but you also have to know when and how to use it. Acquiring that knowledge takes time, and it's essential that you take your time to learn all aspects of drumming so you will be a musician playing the drums, not a person beating the drums.

use contrasting dynamics

Dynamics, loud and soft, add drama to music and give compositions emotional impact. They attract the listener's attention in a very basic way. Using contrasting dynamics (going from soft to loud to soft) is a very good way to communicate. If you are listening to the music you are playing, you will hear places that should be played loudly as well as places that should be played softly. If you listen and respond to the music, your audience will listen and respond to you.

practice dynamics with rudiments

In order to have the technique needed for the effective use of dynamics, practice rudiments and exercises at several different dynamic levels. This will also heighten your awareness of how to use dynamics well.

develop control and intensity

Many exercises for the development of speed require that a certain amount of pressure be used to get a necessary bounce, automatically making you strike the instrument harder thereby producing a louder sound. Try practicing these "louder" exercises softly. It will be very good for your technique and also for muscle control. A good way of doing this is not to allow the sticks to come up more than approximately 2 inches above the playing surface. No matter how strong or how fast you're playing, discipline yourself not to allow the sticks to come up any higher than a couple of inches. This will give you practice in developing the control to play softly yet **with intensity**. It is difficult to play softly without losing the intensity you would get playing louder, and it's precisely the ability to achieve this and other subtle effects that separates the musical drummer from the rest of the pack.

5
READING MUSIC

The demands of today's musical scene make it necessary for drummers to be able to read music. Years ago drummers had to keep time, keep a good musical feeling going, and simultaneously practice the art of concentrated listening, because they were not generally able to read music. Since they weren't playing melodic figures per se, it was possible to get the job done without reading.

Today there are still a few giants in our profession who do not read, but their success is due to recognition of their great individual talents. They are in demand for their own unique contributions. The music they play is more or less written for their own voices, and enough time is allowed for rehearsals so they are comfortable with the music. It would be dangerous for students to use these giants as reasons for not learning to read. It's safer and surer to rely on a good reading foundation.

learn to read music fluently

To learn to read music fluently, practice, practice, practice. It is best to study reading with a teacher so your progress can be monitored, mistakes corrected, and challenges offered. In fact, I recommend studying with a teacher at some time during your pursuit of the drums. It is not necessary for each one of us to re-invent the wheel—it's far better and faster to take advantage of the pool of knowledge that already exists. There are many things a teacher can explain that will prevent faulty or incomplete understanding and the development of bad habits. A bad musical habit is very difficult to correct. It may not be possible to study with a formal teacher regularly because of economic restrictions, but try to get instructions or tips from more experienced drummers whenever possible.

study with a teacher if you can

In written music the relationship of notes to rhythm is mathematical, so **counting is mandatory**. Counting reveals the numerical relationship of the written note to its duration in sound, shows the number of beats in a given note, and the numerical relation of one note to to another. It is imperative to master the discipline necessary to be able to count and to play what you've counted. Many students make the mistake of trying to anticipate what a written piece of music is going to sound like

learn to count

without counting it out, inadvertently distorting the numerical relationship of the note to the proper duration of sound.

Because jazz is a "feeling" music, aspiring drummers in the jazz tradition face a conflict. It is impossible to count and at the same time play with a great deal of feeling and creativity. With practice you will become more astute at counting, so you can little by little begin to eliminate the mechanical aspects of counting and deal more with feeling and creativity.

read by counting, then sing the rhythms

Once the mathematical relationship of the the note is understood, and you can read a musical phrase by counting it, the next step is to listen to how it sounds so you will start hearing the rhythms that the notes make based on their mathematical positioning. A good way to do this is to sing the notes rhythmically. Singing your exercises can be advantageous in another way—because the instrument is not needed, you can practice almost any time or any place. I used to sit in bed at night and instead of reading a book or watching TV, I would read my musical exercises and practice singing them.

This form of practice leads to perfecting the art of sight reading, sight reading being the ability to read a piece of music correctly the first time through. Memorizing basic phrases that will be used over and over, but in different combinations, is the key.

tips on sight reading

For example, write out a measure of four quarter notes in 4/4 time. Because you understand the mathematical relationship of written notes to duration of sound, you know that the four quarter notes will be equal to each other and will sound da-da-da-da-da in whatever tempo you choose. Whenever you see those four quarter notes in that context, you will **immediately** be aware of the rhythm they represent. Gradually write out more complicated rhythms. Later, when you see those memorized groups of notes in various compositions, you won't have to count them out—you'll already know how they sound. The more different groups of notes you are familiar with, the better you'll be able to sight read.

analyze figures

However, even if you've memorized hundreds of note groupings, you won't recognize every figure you see. Writers are always coming up with new figures, or new combinations of familiar figures. But they are all based on groups of notes in mathematical relationships to each other, so even if you are unfamiliar with a figure you should be able to break it down into familiar parts and understand it quickly.

When you study sight reading exercises, first count them out so you are sure of the mathematical and rhythmic relationships. Then sing what you've counted out. Reading and singing music without playing it on your instrument is good practice for sight reading, because you are not hampered by the physical execution of the rhythms.

Although drum music is not written tonally, it is also a good idea to learn to read tonal music as this will further your development as a complete musician.

practice on the drums

Before closing this chapter, I'd like to stress the importance of practicing on the drums themselves whenever possible. I know that because of close living conditions it may be difficult and at times impossible to practice on the drums. But because mastery of this instrument is achieved by complete control of how the stick strikes the drum head to produce the sound, it is mandatory to spend as much time as possible practicing on the drums themselves to acquire that touch and to further train your ears to the sounds of music.

the practice pad

The drum pad, while producing a similar bounce, does not have the same feel or sound as the drum. Only in the repetitive exercises that improve physical technique is the silence of the drum pad desirable. Keep in mind that other instrumentalists such as horn players do not practice on pipes or any other false contrivance that is foreign to the feel and the sound of their instrument. They may be forced to use certain instrumental devices such as mutes or muted keyboards to deal with the noise factor but they are still basically practicing on their instrument. Find a way to practice on your drums. It is **that** important.

practice hand to hand

One more hint—practice all exercises hand to hand. By that I mean leading off with right hand or left hand with an equal amount of expertise. Right handed drummers seem to practice everything leading with the right hand more so than the left, and they will consequently play leading with the right and kind of dragging the left along. The reverse is true of left handed drummers. This habit places limitations both on freedom of movement and individual expression when attempts are made to play around the entire drum set. By developing the skill to lead with either hand, the drummer has the freedom to move to the left or to the right at will, consequently moving up and down the scale intervals created by the tom-toms. This technique is especially valuable in today's drumming, where many toms are used.

Many students have asked me how they can improve their left hand. This ambidextrous approach to practicing will be a major contributing factor. Try to get to the place where you're not thinking left or right handed, but you are free to use either hand with equal ease.

THE IMPORTANCE OF GOOD HEALTH HABITS, MENTAL AND PHYSICAL

A few years ago my good friend Elvin Jones and I happened to be hanging out together, and a group of aspiring young drummers assembled around us. We got into a discussion about the instrument and some of the things that could help drummers play better. As we were talking, someone mentioned that the way we play is affected by the way we think, and that prompted Elvin to remark, "Yes, if you think stupid you play stupid."

think creatively, you will play creatively

That statement reflects a profound truth about creative music because players express their own personalities in their playing. It follows that to improve as a musician one should also pay attention to personality traits that could affect performance, for example, compassion and honesty.

Drummers are called upon to play all types of music with all types of musicians, and because the drums are basically used to accompany, the way the drummer feels about the people influences the way he or she accompanies. Respect others, feel compassion for them, be honest with them. Without compassion and honesty, the drummer may not play to enhance the group's music, especially if he or she is bored or angry. Keep in mind, if boredom sets in while you are playing with creditable musicians,

the drummer must provide inspirational support

it is basically your fault. You're not putting enough concentration into the music to inspire the other musicians, let alone yourself. Providing **inspirational support** for the group is the drummer's responsibility.

Although there are many claims both for and against astrology and it is not considered a proven science, I've found that studying astrology is an interesting way to become more aware of other people's emotions as well as your own, because astrology deals with universal human characteristics. I recommend it as an aid to becoming more in tune with yourself and your your world.

whole body health

Maintaining good physical health is equally important, because the drum is a physical instrument. The whole body is used when playing the drums, so I can't stress too strongly the importance of keeping the whole body in shape. I try to think of myself as an athlete in training while stressing the importance of conditioning. When your body is in good condition, it will feel good to play. No one can perform their best when they're ill, so to speak. The observance of the basic rules of maintaining health through good diet, exercise, and proper rest, in most cases, will suffice.

keep your mind in good shape

The use of stimulants such as barbiturates, narcotics and alcohol should be avoided, because these drugs can and will harm your body. Some of them are harmful immediately, and you'll notice a definite decline in your physical abilities right away; others take longer to have the same effect. I know that it seems like the "in" thing to be involved with drugs, and unfortunately musicians have acquired the reputation of being involved with drugs, but the rewards are small compared to the penalties. You must think beyond the short "high" stimulants can provide.

I feel best when I'm performing—I more or less live to perform. And I know to get that good feeling I must be in shape so I can perform well. The false euphoria produced by use of stimulants is dangerous twofold: it deteriorates the body and creates the delusion that you are performing well, while in reality the opposite may be the case. In addition, the use of stimulants may also bring about mental and spiritual depression which is directly contrary to the feelings necessary to deal with the inspiration aspects of the music.

keep your body in good shape

Keep in shape by doing physical exercises that will help your playing. Strenuous gymnastic exercises such as weight lifting may be good for the body beautiful but they may be dangerous to your playing technique by bringing about a muscle-bound condition which can put limitations on the type of movements necessary for playing the drums.

try dancing

I find that calisthenics and exercises that dancers take are excellent for toning the muscles and tendons that are actually used in drumming. Check out a dance class, even take a class yourself. In dancing, the rhythm that is seen in the movement can be directly related to the rhythm produced by the drummer. This rhythmic relationship makes this type of body maintenance enjoyable and productive.

7
HINTS ON TUNING, MAINTENANCE AND EQUIPMENT

keep your equipment in good shape

It's not necessary to have the most expensive or the newest equipment on the market, but it is necessary to keep the equipment you have in excellent playing condition. Any instrument, whether it is old or new, expensive or inexpensive, will play better if it is kept in good shape. Also, be aware that if your instrument is in bad condition, it will literally fight you when you play it. Overcoming this while dealing with the natural demands of making music on the instrument will cause unnecessary drain on your energy and concentration.

Keep all of the moving parts well oiled: the pedals and the tuning rods, etc. This maintains necessary flexibility of the parts even if (or when) a rusting process begins.

drum heads

Keep good heads on the drum. The construction, size and the material of the shell determine the basic sound of the drum, but the quality of the sound depends on the head. As the heads get worn they get stretched, dented and dirty. Keeping the head clean by occasional washing (don't scrub or use harsh detergents or chemicals) will prolong a crisp sound because dirt build-up will tend to muffle the sound. However, what actually wears the heads out is continuous stretching, which is unavoidable. Every time you tune the drum, or hit it with the stick, the head stretches a little more, and you have to put more tension on the heads to produce the same sound. After a while the head stretches so thin it cannot produce a desirable sound, and it's also more likely to break. Today's heads are very well made and durable and will last quite a while with normal use and proper care. Of course, if you break a head it must be replaced immediately.

Choose the right heads. I find that the thinner the head the better quality of sound it produces, probably because thinner heads vibrate faster and thus resonate more. However, resonance alone is not the only consideration. The batter head, the head we play on, is subject to breakage, so in selecting a batter head you must find one that will be thin enough to produce maximum resonance but still thick enough to provide stretch. For the bottom surface select as thin a head as possible. This will give the drum a wide, open sound. A thick bottom head will produce a muddy, stuffy sound.

In this age of high tech and electronics, an assortment of heads are available for the many special effects found in recording and electronic ensembles—black dots, canosonics, hydraulics, etc. However, you should still approach the selection and tuning of heads in an acoustic manner. Then, depending on the demands of the performance situation or gig, go from there.

tuning the drums

Tune the instrument properly and keep it tuned. If the drum is in tune with itself it will be relatively or compatibly in tune with the instruments we may accompany.

First, tune the drum to itself. Tap the head in front of each tensioning rod, turning the rods until every area produces the same pitch. When the pitch is the same all the way around the head, the drum is in tune with itself.

Next, tune the drum for relative pitch. I find that the bottom head should be fairly tight for a clear, resonant tone. Once the bottom head is tuned to itself with workable tension, tune the top head to the pitch you want, striking the head as you tighten or loosen it and keeping it in tune with itself. Some drummers like the low sound produced by a loose head, and some prefer the higher pitch of a tighter head.

tune to the sound you want

Many drummers make the mistake of tuning the drum by feel. It is easier to play on a looser head than on a tight one, so drummers whose technique needs improving tune loose to match their technical level. This isn't a good practice. Tune the drum to the sound you want and practice to improve your technique.

Some drummers tune to a specific note. The drum cannot be tuned as precisely as a tonal instrument. When the stick strikes the head it will tend to change the pitch slightly. Remember, the drum is not a tonal instrument per se. Also, if the drum is tuned to one note, in one key, it may not sound good when the ensemble changes keys. Rather than tune to a note, tune to a sound that's compatible to the overall sound of the music you'll be playing regardless of changing keys.

The technique of tuning to an overall sound especially applies to the bass drum and tom-toms. The snare drum has a sound of its own which is very personal amongst drummers. I think too much emphasis is put on the importance of the snare drum. From a standpoint of tonality and pitch it is the least musical of the drums that make up the set. Yet many drummers seem to make this the most important of the drums. The great Dizzy Gillespie once asked me "Why do all drummers suffer from snare drumitis?" I don't mean to minimize the importance of the snare drum sound within the framework of the music that the drummer will accompany, but try not to catch snare drumitis.

tuning the bass drum

Because of the function of the bass drum in an ensemble, the drummer must tune for sound and impact as well as a relative pitch. In the studios and in pop/rock music the desired bass drum sound is achieved by a relatively loose batter head, heavily muffled and miked. The drummer in this situation is more or less at the mercy of the sound engineer, but in more acoustical situations, which of course include jazz, it will be up to the drummer to find a compatible bass drum sound through proper tuning. The batter head should be tighter than the front head with just enough muffling to absorb extra overtones. The drummer may want to experiment with the related tensioning of the two heads to acquire the necessary compatible sound and relative pitch, but in most cases the aforementioned head tension relationship will get the job done.

tom-tom intervals

Even though we tune for relative pitch and compatible sound, it is possible and desirable to have scale pitch intervals between the tom-toms. The small tom-tom can be be tuned a perfect fourth higher than the large tom-tom. If there are more than two toms, as is very popular today, they can be tuned a step apart, producing a scale. Any scale pitch intervals can be used depending again on the overall sound of the ensemble that the drums will be accompanying.

single head drums

The single head drum has become very popular, especially in the field of rock music. I prefer drums with two heads because the bottom head controls the timbre and resonance of the drum. One thing that makes the single head drum so popular is its volume—because the drum is wide open (no opposing head or resonating chamber), the sound is louder. However, to my ears, the sound is not as beautiful as the sound produced by a double-headed drum.

cymbals

A word about choosing cymbals. Because of the varying degrees of sound in cymbals of various sizes, the beginning student of the drums may become confused in his or her selection, especially when confronted with escalating prices. It has been my experience that many students really do not know what they want. I find the easiest way to deal with this situation is to get cymbals that sound like the cymbals played by one of your favorite drummers. This will give an inspirational basis to the beginning of finding your own sounds, an ability which only comes with a certain amount of experience. Do not misinterpret this practice to be that of a copycat. There is nothing wrong with plugging into your heroes to find inspiration and a springboard to your own talents as long as you do not let the vastness of their talent and contributions intimidate you.

the drum seat, again

As I mentioned in Chapter 1, the drum seat or throne, as it is called, is actually the most important piece of equipment in the drum set. Remember, the seat must support the body while both arms and and legs are in perpetual motion. This situation makes it imperative that a comfortably soft, very stable and strong seat be used regardless of your budget. Damage to the body, which can be potentially serious, is brought about by sitting on an improper seat over a period of time. All drummers take heed: it is **vital** for your productive longevity.

8
KEEPING TIME
(rhythm is the heart beat of music, and the drum is the heart beat of rhythm)

Two words are often used in connection with rhythm: *time* and *tempo*. **Time** is the steady rhythmic pulse of the music; we tap our feet to it, we dance to it. The word **tempo** refers to the speed of that pulse, ranging from very slow to very fast.

Rhythm is a basic element of music, and a steady rhythm underlies most popular music (rock, gospel, jazz, etc.). In experimental jazz, free improvisation, the trend is away from keeping a steady rhythm or time, but that is the exception, not the rule. Drummers, no matter what kind of music they want to play, must be able to **keep good time**.

keep good time: drummer + group, not drummer only

The ability to keep steady time, to maintain a chosen tempo, must be developed early in a drummer's career, but it is a mistake to think that the drummer alone is responsible for the time in an ensemble. All the members of an ensemble must work together to keep a good time feel. Particularly, the other members of the rhythm section—keyboard and bass, sometimes guitar—must be willing to work towards achieving a similar or compatible conception of time. When they do, the rhythm section jells, as we say. In today's music, the bass anchors the time and the drums color it, so a musical and spiritual marriage between the bass player and the drummer is vital. When everyone in the ensemble is in tune with the time feeling, and when the drummer is swinging and locked in with the bass, that's when the groove really happens, or as we may now say, it's in the pocket.

Often the drummer is blamed when the time fluctuates in an ensemble. This can be the drummer's fault, of course, but it may be the fault of the other members of the rhythm section. Don't automatically take all the blame—it is a group effort.

concentrate
. . . listen
. . . and relax

To keep good time, you must **concentrate**, **listen** and **relax**. Concentrate on the leader's count-off: absorb it, remember it, maintain it. Once the ensemble is into the tune, listen to how the other musicians are handling the time feeling. Concentrate on how the other musicians and **yourself** are maintaining that feeling. Listen to the music that's being played and draw your inspiration and interpretation from it. While you are doing all of this, relax. (Lots of luck!) It's quite a chore, but once the drummer has acquired the discipline necessary to block **everything** out of the mind except the music at hand, allowing full concentration on what he or she hears, the chore actually becomes very simple.

tempos can vary

In considering the tempo of a piece of music, be aware that tempos do sometimes vary during performance depending on the feelings of the musicians involved. The variations are usually slight: a tune may start off at one tempo and gradually settle into another tempo, either faster or slower, because the ensemble collectively feels more comfortable with the new tempo. It is rare for anyone to object when this happens collectively because our music is based on a combination of feeling and precision. If the new tempo allows the ensemble to lock into a more comfortable groove, then it is the right tempo. Variations in tempo that are considered incorrect occur when the leader's tempo is not followed and one musician or section causes the tempo to slow down or speed up.

To improve your time feeling while practicing alone, practice with a metronome, a click track if available, or play along with some form of recorded music. While playing along with these devices, practice the aforementioned total concentration on what you are hearing. Continue this practice of total concentration on what you hear while playing for the rest of your life. It is the key to good accompaniment, which is what this instrument that we are discussing is all about.

watch out for speed

Any mention of speed or playing fast can be a dangerous subject with drummers, especially young, high-energy, aspiring drummers. This happens to be an on-going problem because it seems at times that every drummer's major goal in life is to fly around the drums with little or no consideration for the other important dimensions of musical taste. However, a complete musical message includes phrases, melodies, figures and tempos of various speeds, therefore it is incumbent upon the student drummer to develop the ability to express all of these dimensions, including speed, without becoming one of those basic deaf speed freaks.

to play fast, practice slowly

In the music of jazz the drummer will have to deal with many different tempos, in some cases incredibly fast tempos. I find the best way to practice this is to play a given tempo as fast as you can play it convincingly and relaxed. Then, increase the tempo slightly. Stay at that tempo until you have perfected this new, slightly faster tempo (convincingly and relaxed). Continue this line of practice, gradually increasing the tempo while you continue to achieve clarity and relaxation. Do **not** jump to a tempo that is obviously too fast for your abilities. It will be a waste of time because you will be struggling, and you may adopt bad habits brought on by tension and inability. This same step-by-step system of gradually increasing speed of playing can be applied to any type of exercise where speed is desired. Just remember, do not attempt the new tempo or speed until the previous one has been perfected with complete relaxation.

try to practice with a bass player

Earlier in this chapter I mentioned playing along with a metronome or some type of recording for the practice of keeping time. Along with whatever is available in recording material, I suggest that the aspiring drummer try to practice with a bass player whenever possible. It is also very productive to record some rhythmic bass lines to play along with. This can serve as a more musical alternative to the metronome.

THE ART OF LISTENING

An aspiring musician must become proficient in several technical areas, such as reading music and acquiring facility on the instrument, but without the proper audio connection, without really becoming involved with the art of listening, mastery of technique will mean little when it comes to the point of it all—**trying to make music as a successful accompanist in an ensemble**.

can you listen?

It is surprising how many people, musicians included, don't know how to listen. They hear, but they don't listen. The way people have conversations can be a prime example. One person will be making a statement or a point. The alleged listener will be forming a rebuttal before the other person has completed the statement. Consequently the listener stands a good chance of missing much of the subject matter by not actually listening. The thought process used in forming the rebuttal interferes with the concentration necessary for complete listening. Think back to some of your own conversations and I'm sure you will know what I'm talking about. We are all capable of doing this, but now that we have brought it out into the open, we should be able to correct it.

if you can't, watch out

This is exactly what happens when drummers play in a manner that is unacceptable to the ensemble. The drummer is making statements before listening to what he or she is actually accompanying. Learn to **listen correctly**—concentrate completely on what you are hearing without allowing any unrelated thought or outside activity to interfere.

practice listening

Start developing your ear immediately by listening to other drummers and musicians. Every drummer, every musician, starts this way. Even the great innovators had to start somewhere. If you listen to the early records of almost any of the innovators in our music, you will hear the influence of the masters who came before them. You must also listen to live music as often as possible, as well as recorded music.

10
THE ART OF ACCOMPANIMENT

listen to all the melodies

As you should have gathered from the last chapter, the secret to being a good accompanist lies in being an excellent listener. Since the trap drums' primary function is to accompany the ensemble, listening to the ensemble playing the melody is first and foremost. The basic way for the drummer to accompany the melody is to keep the basic beat. In jazz, the drummer also makes intermittent rhythmically melodic statements to accompany the melodies of the ensemble as well as the improvised melodies of the soloists, As a result, concentrated listening is not only important, it is imperative.

know form and melody

In order to accompany any ensemble effectively, the drummer must know the form of the composition and the melody. Knowledge of the harmonic structure, commonly referred to as chord changes, is not totally necessary, but in the highly creative area of jazz music, that knowledge would be a plus.

jazz forms

There are several common composition structures, or forms, used in jazz: one you will often hear is called "rhythm." A rhythm tune has 32 bars made up of four 8-bar phrases. The first two phrases and the last phrase are basically the same while the 3rd phrase, which is called the bridge, has a different melody and chord progression. In musical shorthand this form is AABA. Another common form is the "blues." The blues consists of 12 bars made up of three 4-bar phrases. Each phrase has a different harmonic basis. The entire twelve bars is called a chorus, as is the 32 bars of a rhythm tune. There are many other forms besides those mentioned above.

enhance the music

The drummer must not only be aware of the form, but must use individual creativity to enhance it. This is done by inserting short rhythmically melodic statements in certain places within the structure. These rhythmically melodic statements are commonly known as fills, lead-ins, or breaks. The *fill* is a statement made by the drummer to fill up a hole or to accompany a pause in the melodic phrasing. A *lead-in* is a statement that is so called because it does just that: it leads into the next phrase. At no time should these statements be misconstrued by the drummer as short solos. A solo statement has an entirely different

fill <u>some</u> of the holes

fills are not short solos

musical meaning. The melodic content of the fill or lead-in should be based on the drummer's conception of what he or she hears, which in this case is the melody and form of a given arrangement.

As a matter of fact, any statement made by the drummer should always be stimulated or inspired by what he or she hears. Too often drummers will make statements with little or no awareness of what they should be listening to. This is poor accompaniment. When backing the soloists, base your statements on the way the soloists plays the form. This means laying down a good time feeling and then letting what you hear from the soloist and the rest of the rhythm section dictate your accompanying rhythmic statement. Remember, accompanying a soloist will be like having a conversation. The soloist has the floor, while the drummer listens and interjects rhythmic statements as part of the conversation.

know chord changes, be more creative

Although as I mentioned earlier on, knowledge of the harmonic structure of compositions is not totally necessary, but because of the repetitive manner in which compositions are performed, with various soloists taking many choruses, knowing the chord changes helps the drummer to play with more imagination and creativity. Remember, the soloist is playing chorus after chorus of phrases based on the melody and harmonic structure with accompaniment from the keyboard, bass, and in many cases, guitar. Listening to the way the various musicians deal with the harmonic structure can provide musical reasons for the use of the different colors available on the drum set: tom-toms, cymbals, etc.

read with your ears open

When a drum part is available, you must read with your ears as well as your eyes. The part provides a quick overall view of the form and phrase structure and will usually indicate any unison ensemble passages. However, the drummer will often be expected to play fills, breaks, and set-ups that are not written, so you will be using the part as a sketch or rhythmic guide only.

11
DISCUSSING ENSEMBLE ACCOMPANIMENT
(revised from *Hints on Big Band Drumming*, Modern Drummer Magazine)

keep listening

The main difference between the large ensemble (big band) and small groups is obviously the number of instruments. The conventional big band consists of four or five trumpets, four or five trombones, five reeds or woodwinds, and rhythm section. In any given arrangement, whether the sections are playing independently or together, they will all be playing in the same time or tempo. Now every musician in an ensemble has his or her own conception of where the feeling of the time is. It is incumbent upon the drummer to blend these various time feelings together on his own. This is done by guess what?. . . **L-I-S-T-E-N-I-N-G**. Listening with respect for, but not being intimidated by, the various time feelings. The band will not groove until these individual conceptions are blended into one. So for the drummer, the basic difference between large and small groups is the number of time feelings that he must blend with his own. It can be quite a chore because the drummer often feels outnumbered. Tonal instrumentalists beware. You can intimidate the drummer and affect his or her feeling and creativity. You must listen to the drummer's time feel with the **same respect** that the drummer listens to yours.

inspire the ensemble

It is considered the drummer's responsibility to hold everything together. This is a misconception. It is the drummer's responsibility to inspire everyone to hold it together themselves.

Another difference between large and small ensembles is that, in the small ensemble, every musician knows the tune: melody, the harmonic changes, the rhythms and in most cases something about the story of the composition. Therefore, their whole approach to the music is more relaxed. This related feeling is transmitted to the drummer and vice versa, making the small ensemble sound relaxed or loose. In the big band, aside from the composer and/or conductor, very few, if any, of the musicians have this same full knowledge. Section players, lacking full knowledge of the music yet trying to bring about musical togetherness within their sections, feel that they must depend upon the drummer for time. This can make the drummer

learn the music

feel outnumbered and brings about the tension that gives the big band a stiffer rhythmic feeling. To deal with this the drummer should make every effort to gain the same knowledge of the composition as the composer or conductor. As writing is one of the accepted devices of transmitting that knowledge, the drummer must be a good reader. Being able to hear and repeat melodies quickly is also important.

rhythmic variations can be valid

Maintaining a good time feeling does not mean the drummer has to hammer out the basic cymbal beat all night. What it does mean is that the rhythmic variations be equally as strong or feel just as inspired to the listener as the basic beat. Keep in mind that any variation from the basic cymbal rhythm must have a melodic, rhythmic and emotional reason. Otherwise the variations are likely to be tasteless interruptions of the arrangements.

There are three basic situations in the big band where the drummer may tastefully deviate from the cymbal beat:

making cuts

1. The drummer may play, suggest or interpret a phrase simultaneously with the ensemble. This is commonly known as making cuts with the band.

fills

2. The drummer may play fills written for the drums, commonly known as filling up the holes.

3. The drummer may play improvised fills that are not written but the fills must be placed where they will enhance certain passages within the arrangement.

Let us now discuss these three situations in detail. In playing figures or making cuts with the band, the drummer should be keenly aware of the highs and lows in the melodic content of the phrase and also of the placement of long and short sounds within the melody line. In 4/4 time the eighth note gets one half of a beat: a short sound. A quarter note gets a whole beat: also a short sound, but fuller and fatter than the eighth note. Dotted quarter notes, eighth notes, eighth notes tied together or tied to quarter notes, half notes and whole notes are long sounds. To play a long sound on the drums, play a roll or strike the cymbal. The cymbal should be punctuated with the bass drum or the snare drum, depending on the pitch of the sound. I prefer the sound of the bass drum accent accompanying the cymbal crash. It provides a bottom for the band and gives weight to the sound of the band.

In playing fills with the band, whether written or improvised, the drummer should never think of these orchestral situations as short solos. They are rhythmically melodic statements that should enhance the melody of the phrase. The drummer should be stimulated and inspired by what the ensemble plays both before and after the fill, making the fill a legitimate and timely comment.

A written fill is notated on the drum part. It is a short space, usually one or two measures, sometimes three or four, and is indicated by the word "fill." The content of the fill, or drum statement, is left to the drummer's imagination.

An improvised fill is not indicated on the part. The drummer is free to choose not only what he plays, but also when he plays. As in the written fill, however, the drum statement should be based on what the ensemble is playing and on the written drum part.

you lead the way

One of the most important effective improvised fills is called a lead-in. It leads the band into the next passage. A lead-in helps to keep the band aware of the structure of the composition while inspiring their entrances. The crescendo pressed roll popularized and masterfully played by Art Blakey is an example of a very effective fill. Mr. Blakey was without a doubt one of the true pioneering geniuses in the evolution of this instrument and a formidable big band drummer. In making lead-ins and fills, drummers have a tendency to be brass-conscious and at times not give enough listening attention to what the reeds are doing. Many times composers will have the reed section playing a melody to bring in the brass. A good musical lead-in by the drummer must accompany, not wipe out, this statement by the reeds. Another example of the value of listening: remember, drummers, read with your ears as well as your eyes.

read with eyes and ears open

All drummers have favorite licks, so when the creative juices aren't flowing they can fall back on the familiar. This is fine as long as the lick fits by rhythmically enhancing the melody. These licks, or for that matter any rhythmic statement other than the basic beat should never be forced. Let what you hear based on knowledge of the tune inspire your statements.

the drum solo

Drum solo situations in the big band are just about the same as in the small band. In the case of a long solo the drummer is free to develop many different ideas, but he or she must stay in touch with the structure of the tune and still try to communicate with the audience. For short solos positioned within the arrangement, the drummer may include some of the ingredients of the aforementioned fills. Soloing on the closing chord of an exciting arrangement is an effective device used by many drummers. This can be fun and very gratifying, but it should be done in good taste with sensitivity to the timbre, volume and quality of the sound of the chord. Many drummers, after butchering an arrangement, will really lay into the last chord, as if to make amends.

bigger isn't louder, it's stronger

Hypothetically a major factor separating big band playing from small group accompaniment is dynamics of sound, the conception being the more horns, the louder the drummer must play. Not true. The more instruments, the **stronger** the drummer must play for reasons already mentioned. Dynamics, whether to play loud or soft, must be dealt with in any size ensemble. The dynamic level of the drummer's sound must accompany that of the ensemble.

sit where you can hear everyone

In order to play your best in a big band you must be able to hear every section. The drummer should sit where this is acoustically possible and be provided with a monitor speaker if necessary. The following diagram illustrates the set up that I prefer. Notice that the drums are located in the middle of the band.

OVERHEAD VIEW

keep learning

As you should have gathered by now, the differences between accompanying a large ensemble and a small ensemble have been heretofore grossly exaggerated, mainly because we are all still learning about this instrument, the traps or multiple percussion, the newest and only instrument conceived to play jazz.

12
THE WARM UP EXERCISE

I have put together some very interesting exercises using stickings inclusive of some rudiments. I call this the "Warm Up Exercise." The basic function of this exercise is that the drummer can gradually increase and decrease hand speed while still maintaining a steady tempo with the bass drum and hi-hat. This is very important because a good drummer must be able to maintain a steady tempo regardless of hand speed, except in free form music where a steady tempo is not always desired. But again, a good drummer must have a good time feeling.

In practicing this exercise, think rhythmically. Don't get so involved with the sticking that you lose the rhythm of the groups of notes relating to the tempo. Be conscious of the subdivisions of the beat. Use a metronome or some form of rhythmic accompaniment.

Practice for maximum relaxation and control, not speed. Let the speed come naturally. Try this exercise in different tempos, but begin with a slow tempo. Remember, it takes more control to stay slow. Keep the same tempo and dynamic level for the entire page.

Also, practice this exercise with both *right hand* and *left hand* lead. By today's standards of popular music a drummer should become as ambidextrous as possible.

Keep steady rhythm with the feet. I will suggest a few different foot rhythms later (see page 51), but for now just use the basic four beats to the bar on the bass or kick drum with the hi-hat on two and four.

Be sure that all of the transitions, going from one group of notes to the next, are smooth and in time.

Repeat each two measure phrase four times, then go on to the next line. Once you have mastered a whole page or set, try it with a different tempo and dynamic level. Suggested metronome markings: ♩ = 72, ♩ = 102, ♩ = 192; suggested dynamic levels: *p mf f*.

Remember, do not change the tempo or dynamic level during the playing of a page. For maximum benefit, all the aforementioned elements must be perfected.

You are now ready to begin. Right hand lead sticking is on the top line; left hand lead sticking is shown underneath it. Do not change lead while playing this exercise. Play the entire page with right hand lead, then do the page with left hand lead as notated. When these stickings have been perfected on one drum or drum pad, the toms can be included.

Sets 1, 2 and 3 should be played evenly, without accents. Try to feel the rhythmic flow of the groups of notes. Repeat each two-measure phrase four times.

Set 1

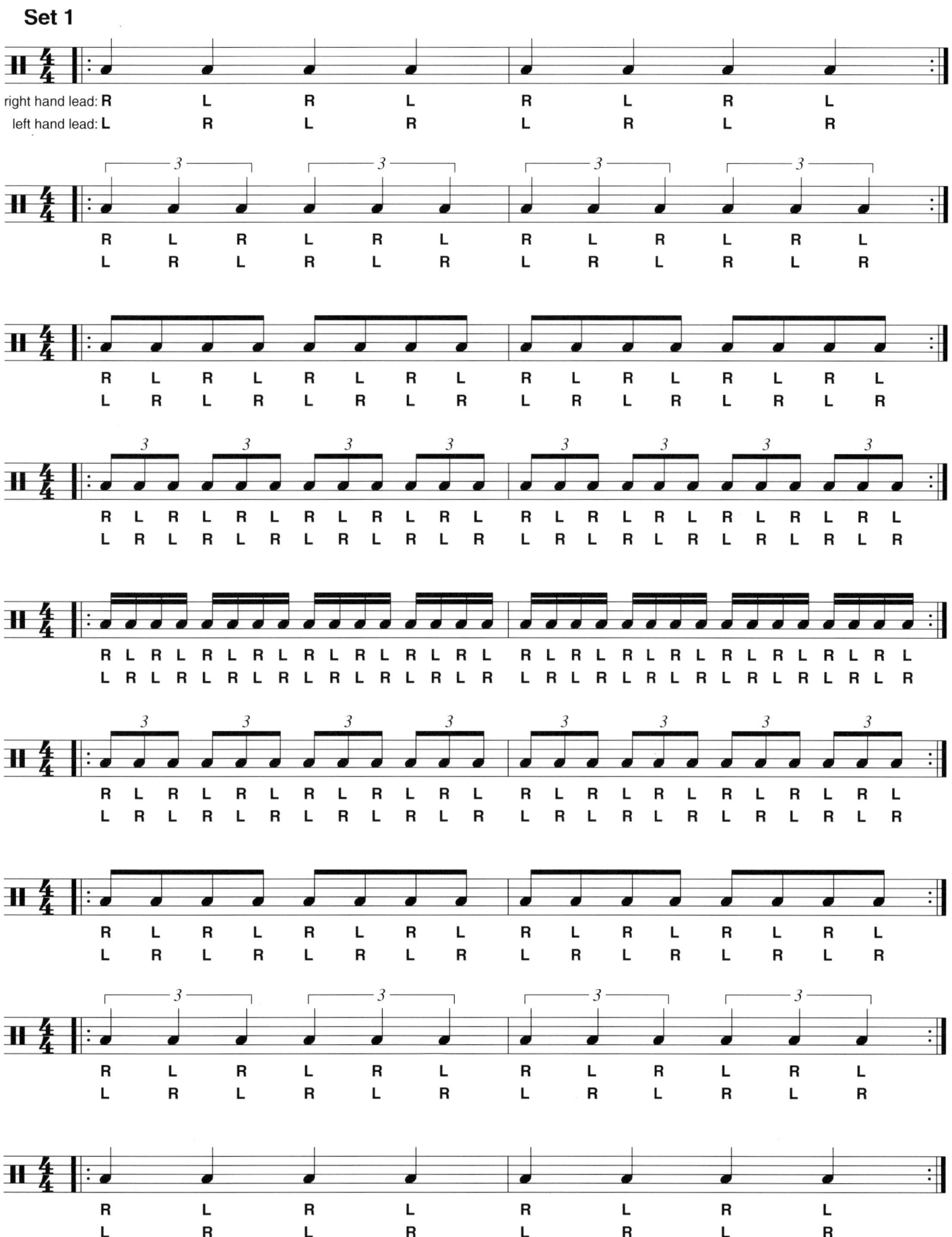

Set 2

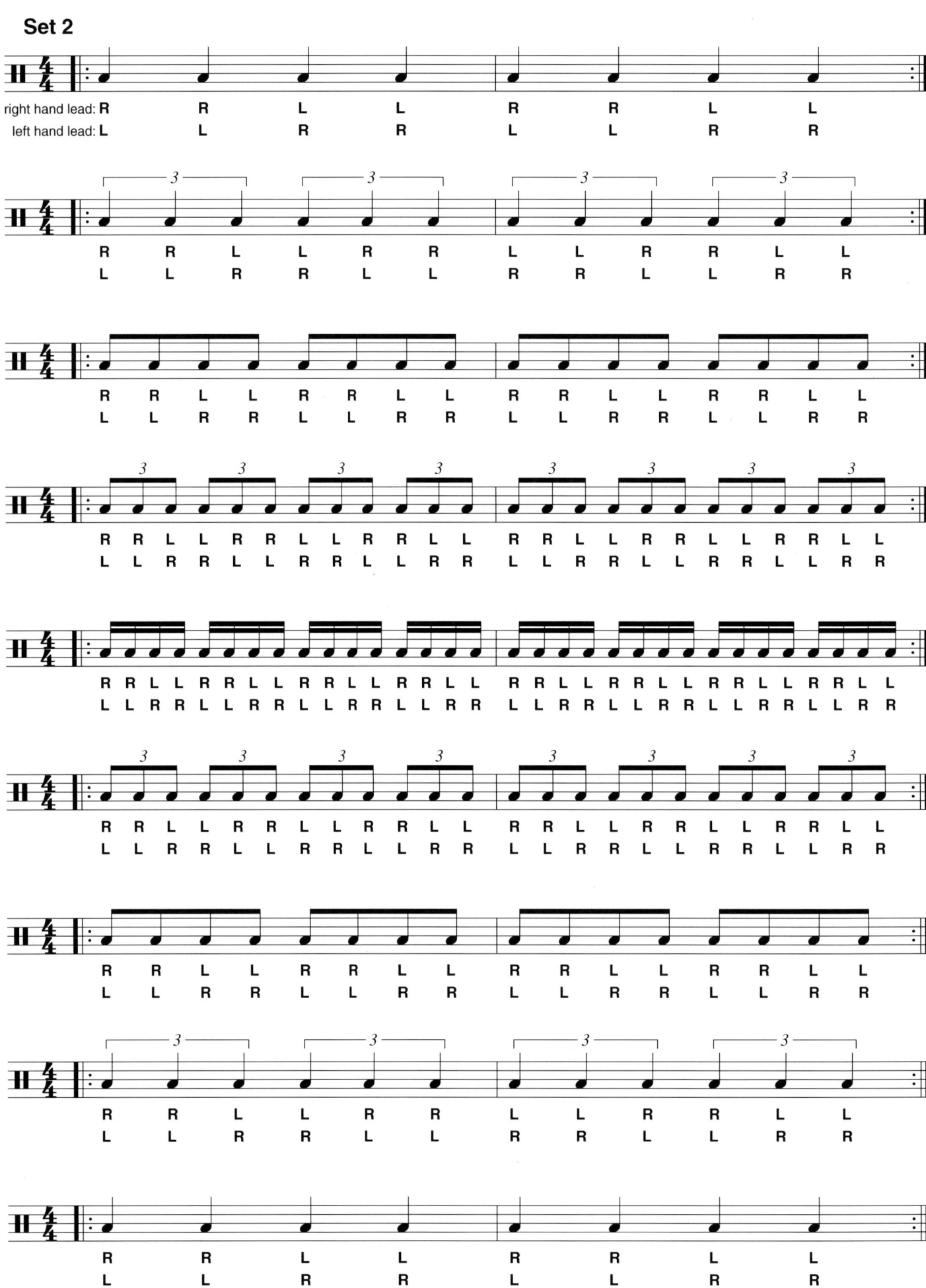

When playing quarter note triplets with a paradiddle sticking, it will take 4 bars for the sticking to resolve back to the lead hand. Consequently, I have written out four bars for those lines in this and the following exercises. Repeat the 4-measure lines once to complete an 8-measure phrase.

Remember, sticking for both right & left-hand leads are notated but again, do not change leads during the playing of the exercise.

Set 3

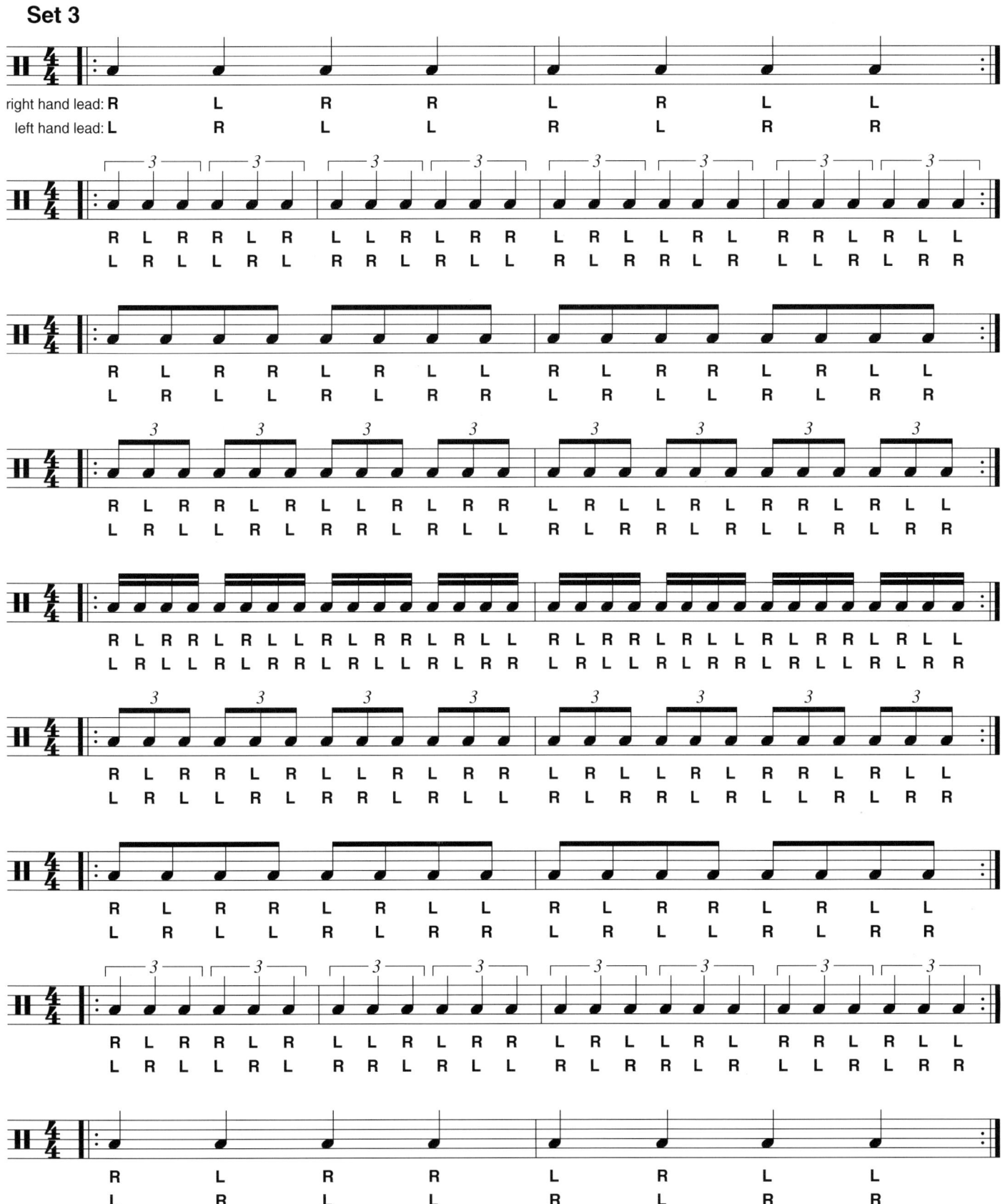

Set 4 introduces accented stickings. Once you have perfected utilizing the accents while playing on one drum or pad, you are ready to play the accented notes on the toms. Play right-hand accents on the floor tom and play left-hand accents on the small rack tom. If you are using a kit with two rack toms you can incorporate them at your own choice. You will find the different tonalities will suggest some interesting rhythmic patterns.

Set 4

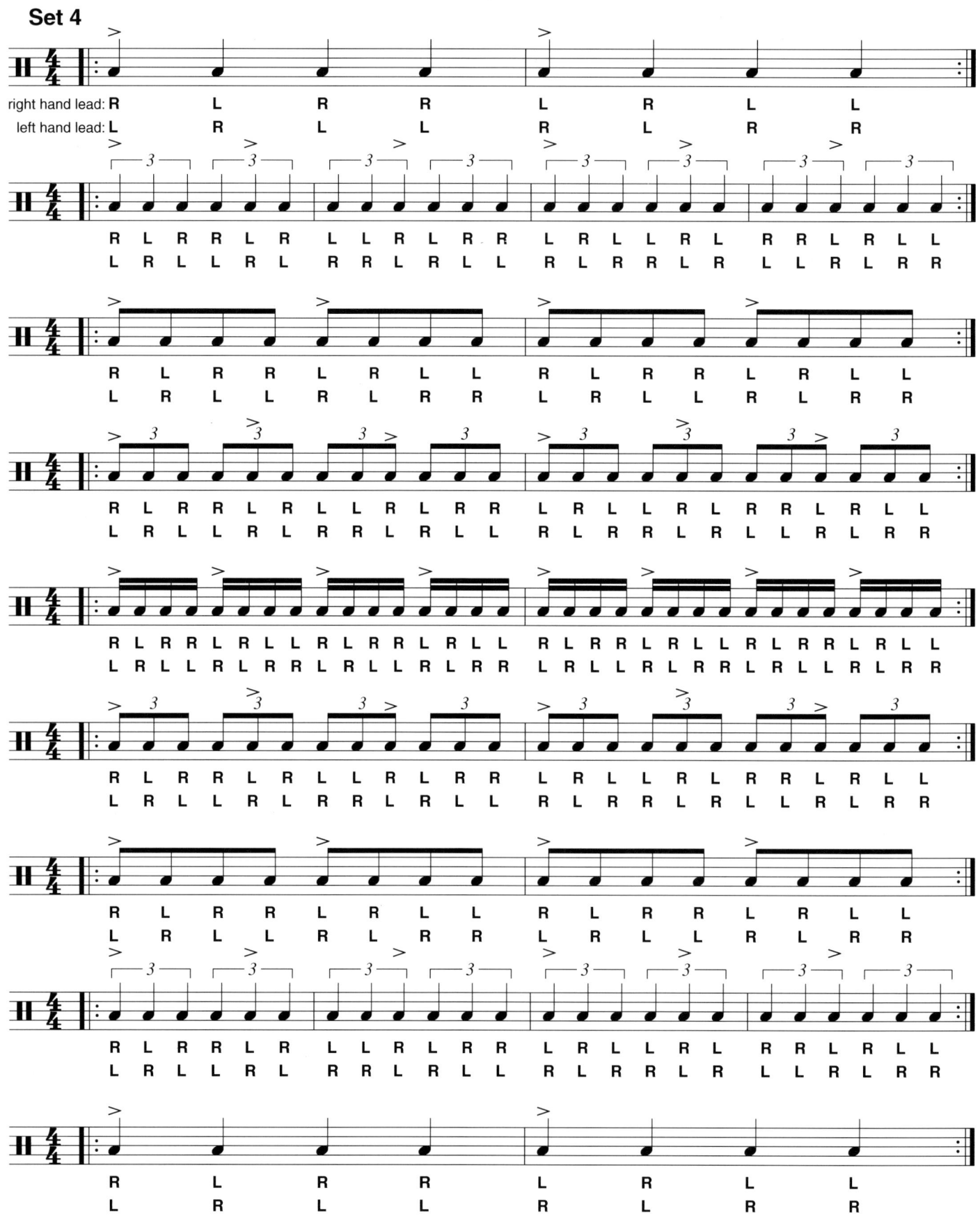

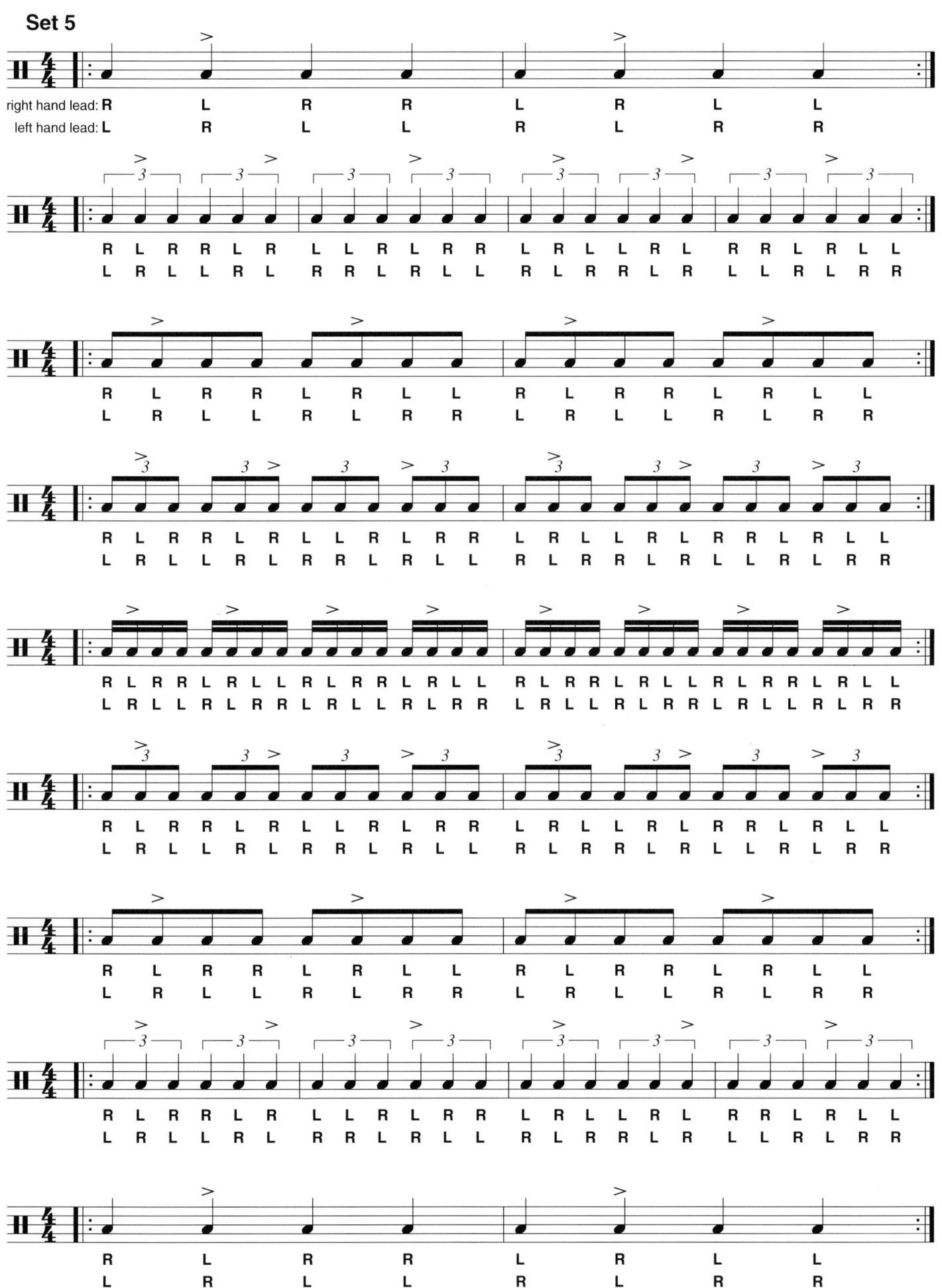

Set 6

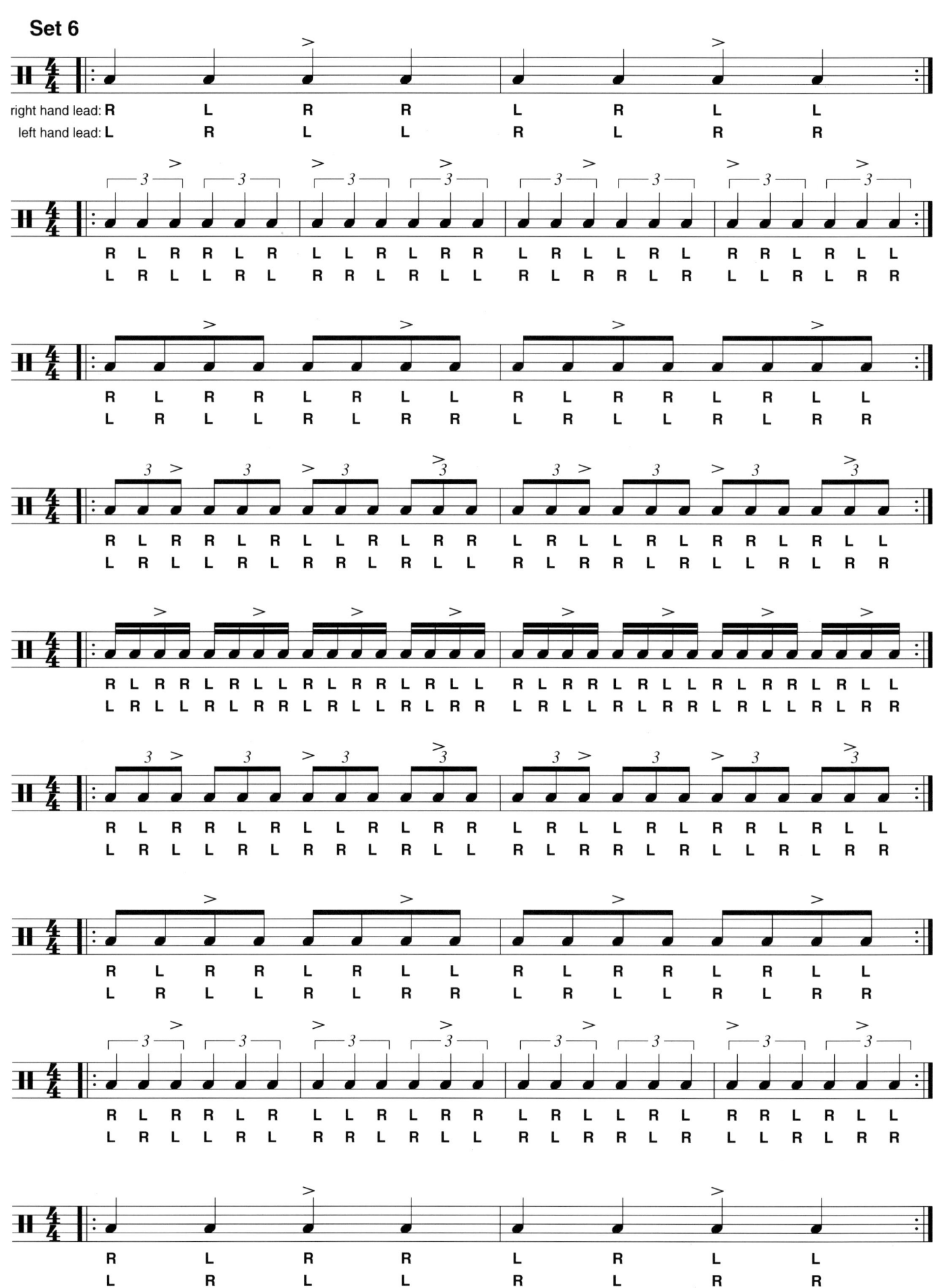

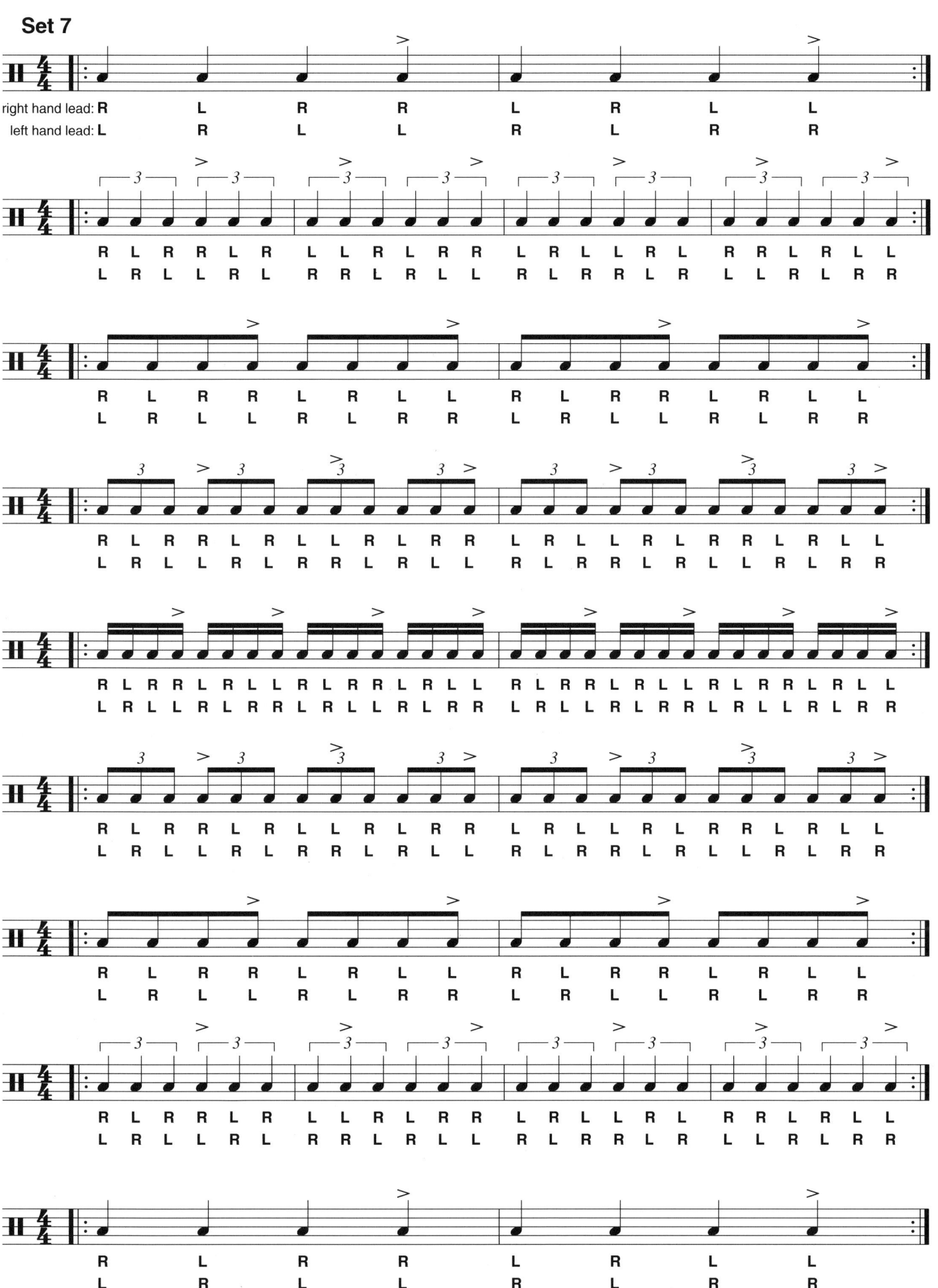

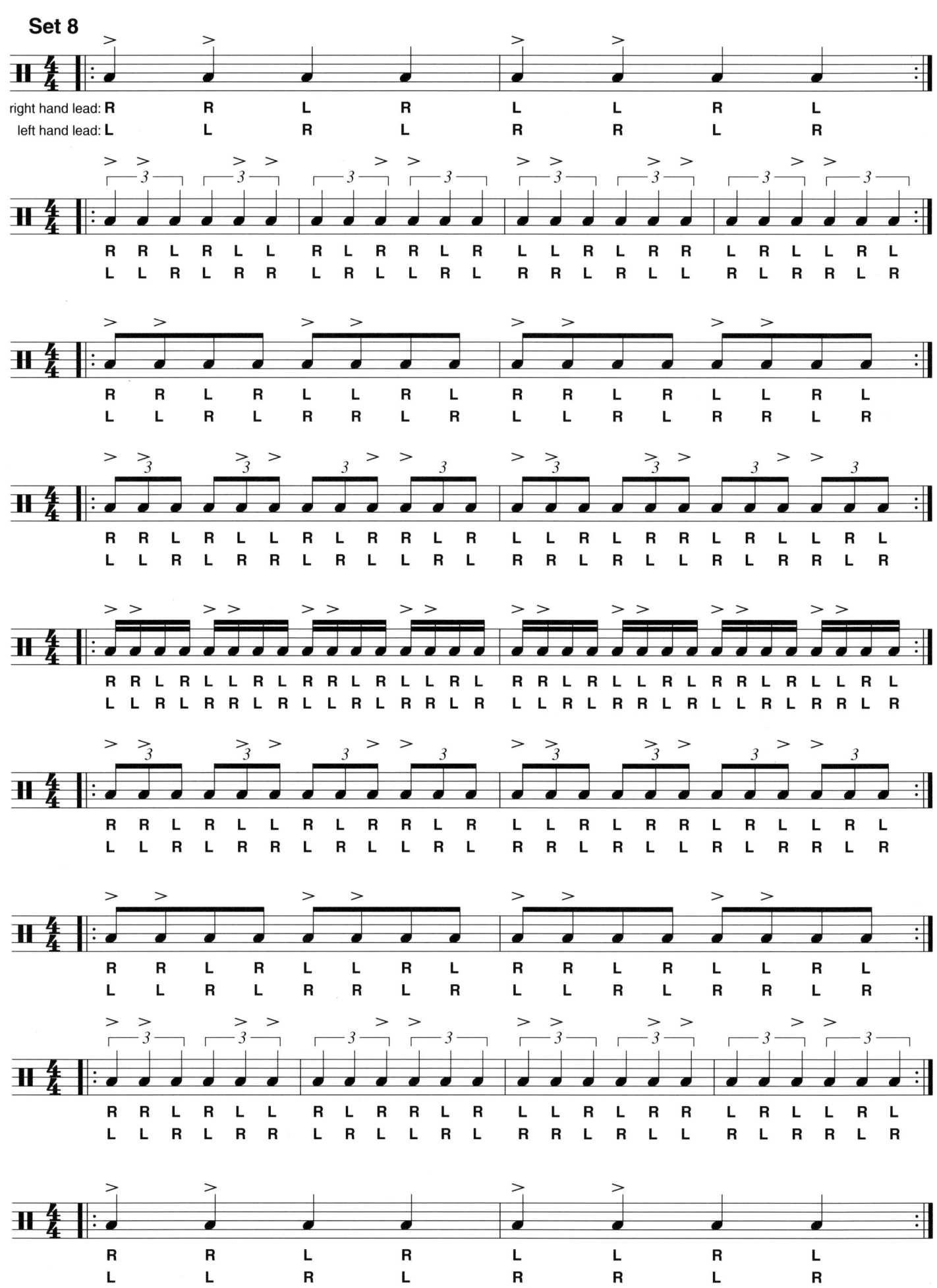

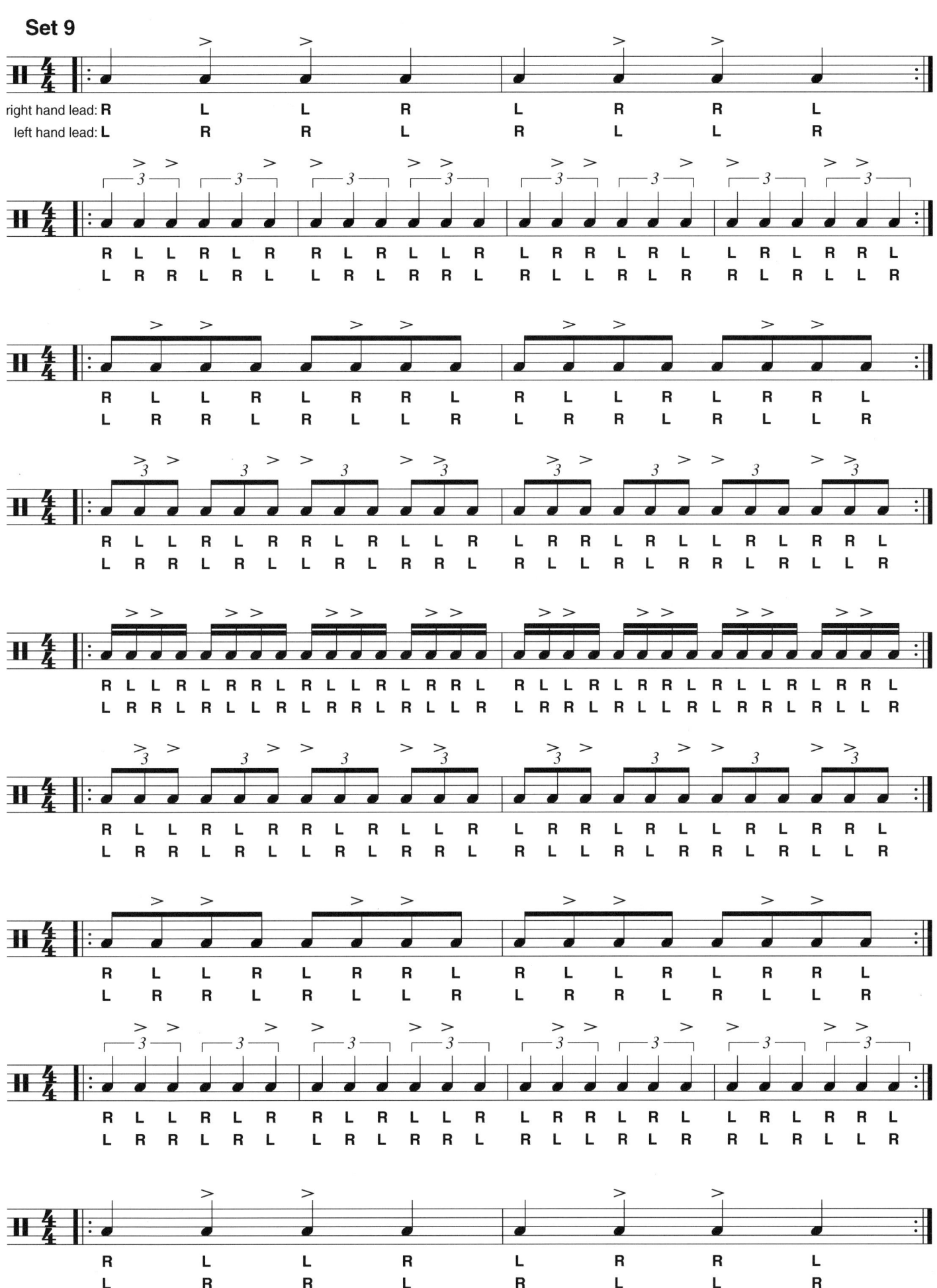

Set 10

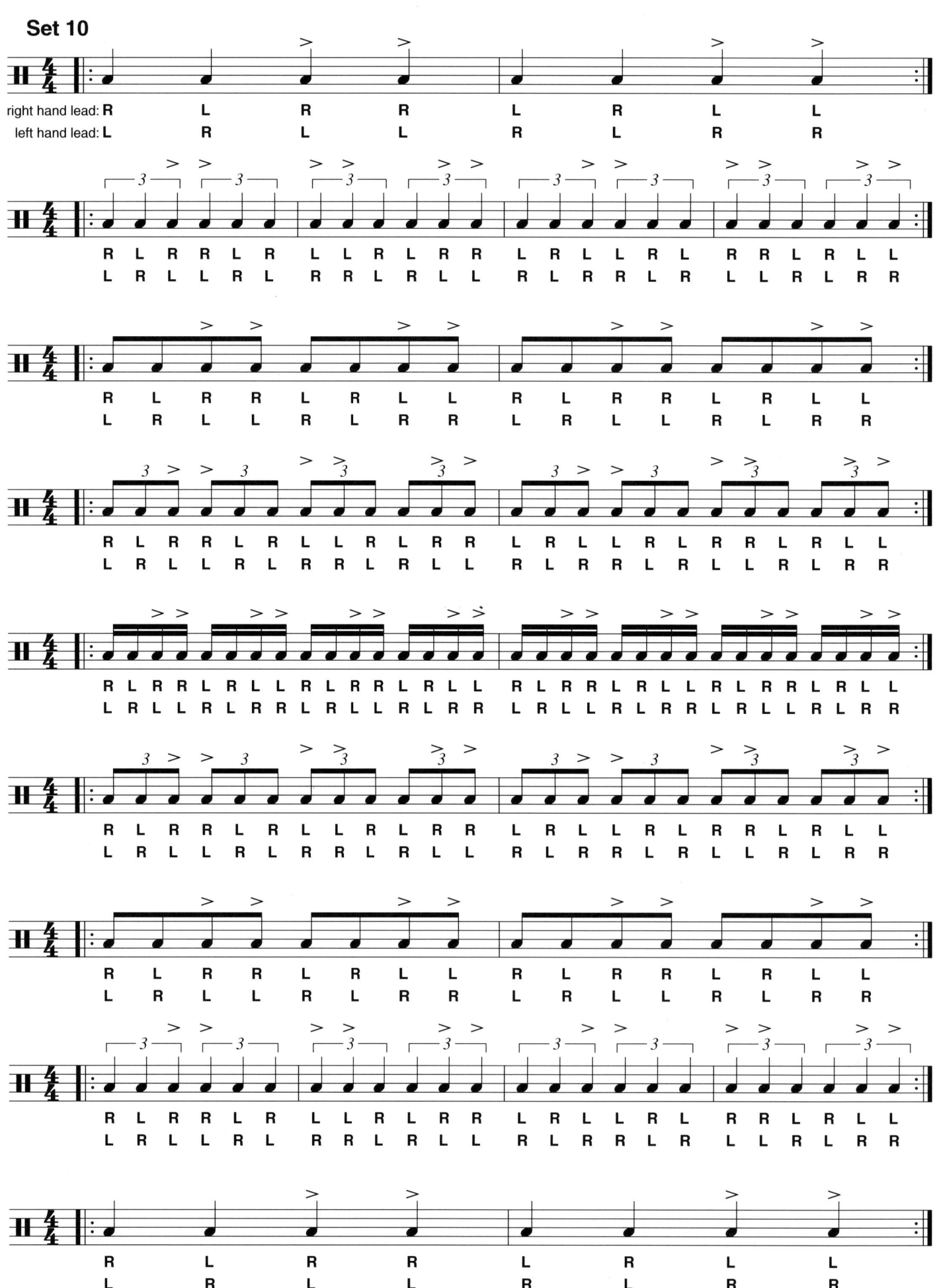

Bass Drum And Hi-Hat Patterns

After perfecting the entire Warm Up Exercise with the basic bass drum and hi-hat pattern, try some of the other variations on this page. However, I would suggest not trying any other patterns until you are completely comfortable with the first or basic bass drum and hi-hat pattern.

THE WARM UP EXERCISE 51

Introducing The Flam

The flam is introduced here using the first line of each set. Apply the flam to all of the exercises of each set once you've mastered the first line. As with all of the other exercises, include either the basic bass drum and hi-hat pattern or some variation of it.

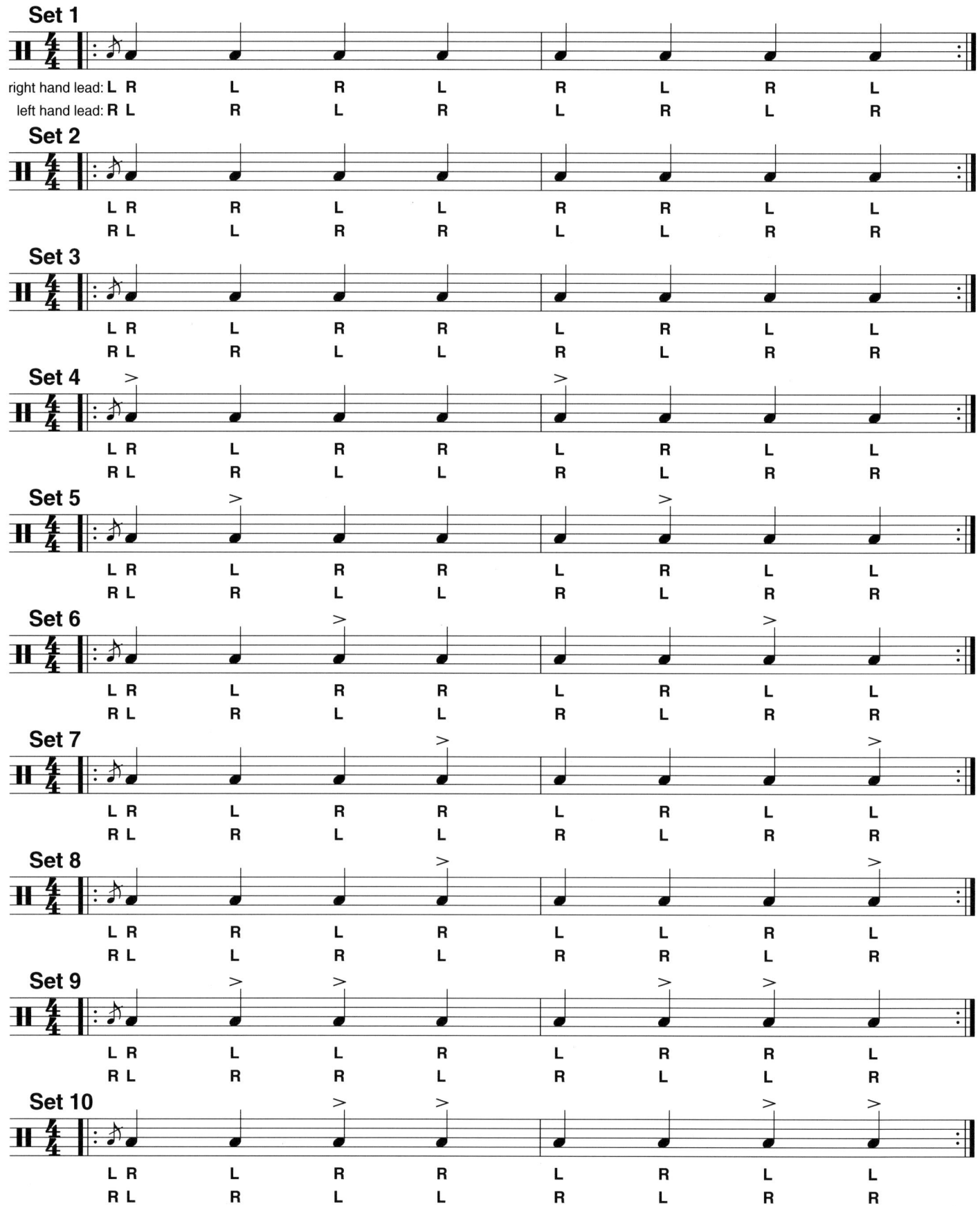

Study In Flam Continuity

Play quarter notes with either foot. Start with a tempo of ♩ = 112. Once you've perfected the 4-measure, 2-measure and 1-measure patterns at ♩ = 112, try faster, more challenging tempos.

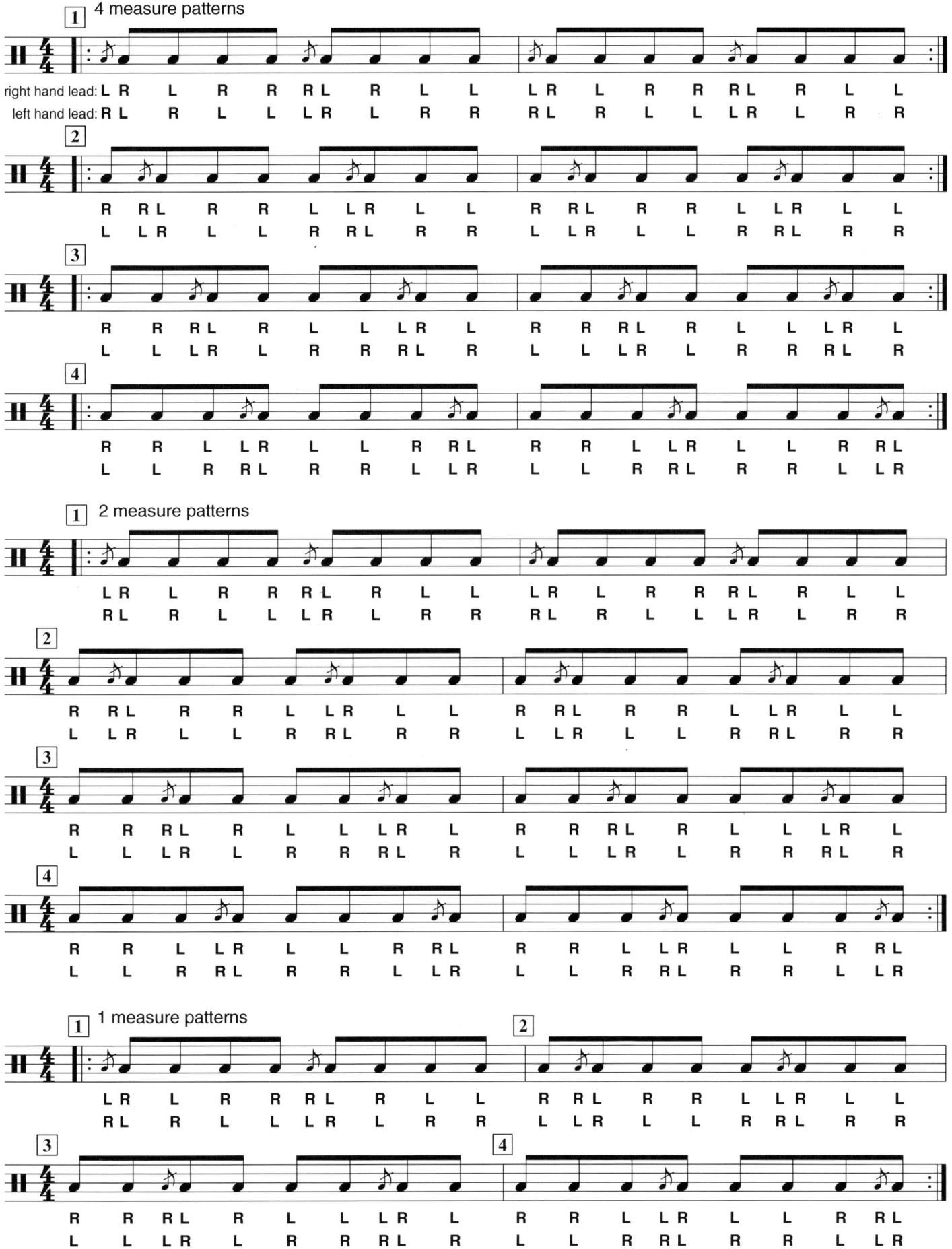

Suggested Flam Sticking

You can play the Warm Up Exercise with flam sticking. I've shown suggested stickings for eighth notes and eighth note triplets using the 2 measure patterns from page 53. You can also experiment with flam and stroke sticking and with feint and flam sticking as I've illustrated on the next page.

Flam Paradiddle with the Flam inversions

right hand lead: L R L R R R L R L L   L R L R R R L R L L
left hand lead: R L R L L L R L R R   R L R L L L R L R R

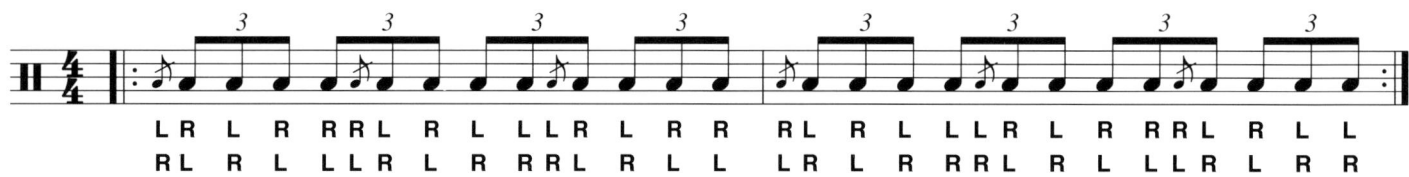

L R L R R R L R L L L R L R R   R L R L L L R L R R R L R L L
R L R L L L R L R R R L R L L   L R L R R R L R L L L R L R R

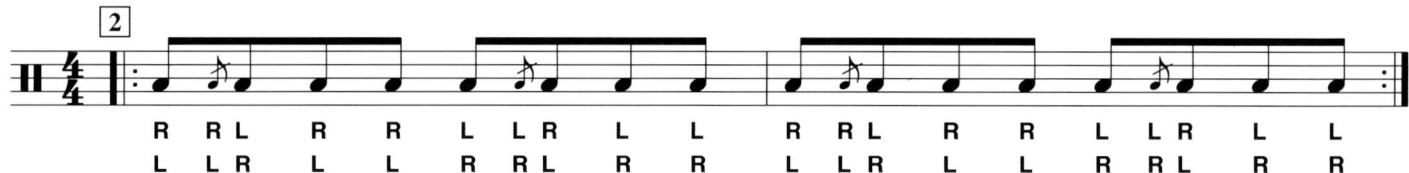

R R L R R L L R L L   R R L R R L L R L L
L L R L L R R L R R   L L R L L R R L R R

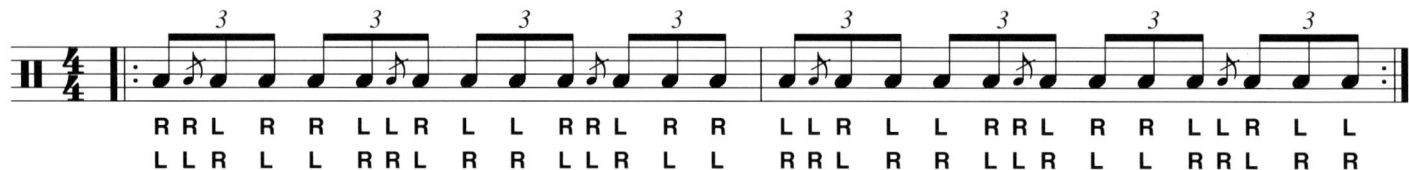

R R L R R L L R L L R R L R R   L L R L L R R L R R L L R L L
L L R L L R R L R R L L R L L   R R L R R L L R L L R R L R R

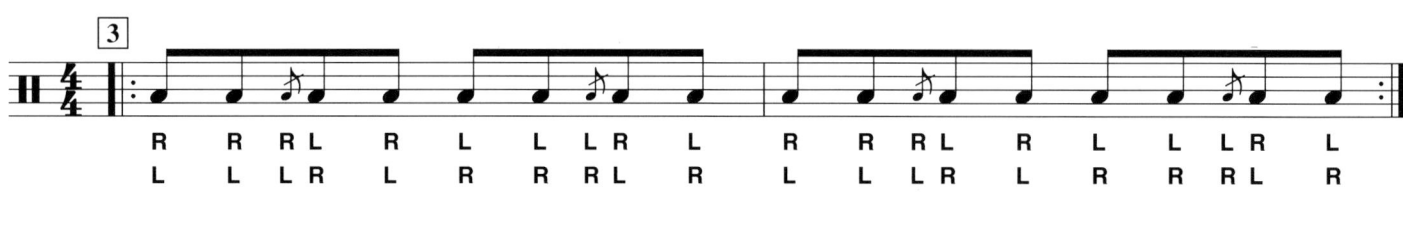

R R R L R L L L R L   R R R L R L L L R L
L L L R L R R R L R   L L L R L R R R L R

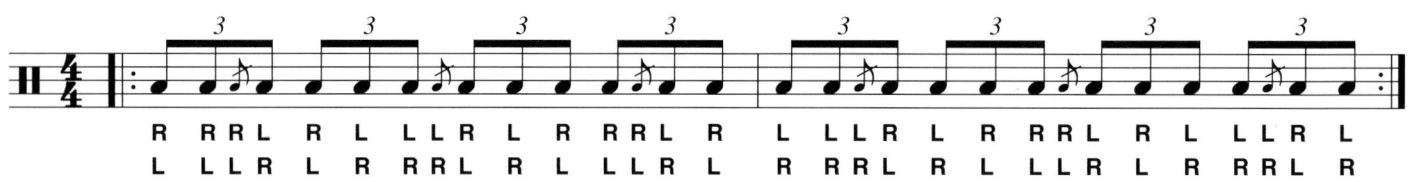

R R R L R L L L R L R R R L R   L L L R L R R R L R L L L R L
L L L R L R R R L R L L L R L   R R R L R L L L R L R R R L R

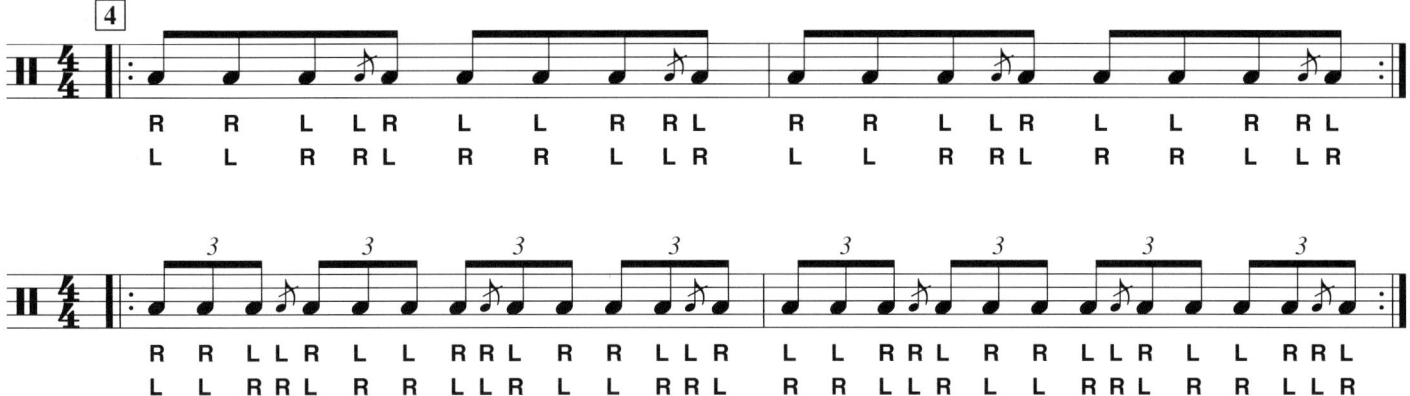

Flam and Stroke

Feint and Flam